Career Launcher

Manufacturing

Career Launcher series

Career Launcher

Manufacturing

Manya Chylinski

Checkmark Books®
An imprint of Infobase Publishing

Career Launcher: **Manufacturing**

Copyright © 2010 by Infobase Publishing, Inc.

Checkmark Books
An imprint of Infobase Publishing
132 West 31st Street
New York NY 10001

Library of Congress Cataloging-in-Publication Data

Chylinski, Manya.
    Manufacturing / by Manya Chylinski ; foreword by Robert W. Hall.
        p. cm. — (Career launcher)
    Includes bibliographical references and index.
    ISBN-13: 978-0-8160-7968-1 (hardcover : alk. paper)
    ISBN-10: 0-8160-7968-4 (hardcover : alk. paper)
    ISBN-13: 978-0-8160-7990-2 (pbk. : alk. paper)
    ISBN-10: 0-8160-7990-0 (paperback : alk. paper)
1. Manufacturing industries—Vocational guidance. I. Title.
    HD9720.5.C52 2010
    338.0023—dc22

                                                                2009029547

You can find Ferguson on the World Wide Web at http://www.fergpubco.com

Produced by Print Matters, Inc.
Text design by A Good Thing, Inc.
Cover design by Takeshi Takahashi
Cover printed by Art Print Company, Taylor, PA
Book printed and bound by Maple Press, York, PA
Date printed: July 2010

Printed in the United States of America

10 9 8 7 6 5 4 3 2 1

This book is printed on acid-free paper.

Contents

Foreword

When I got my first paycheck from a factory 55 years ago, the shop was run by a big electric motor that drove a power shaft in the middle of the room, powering all the machines with belts. Even then it was an antiquated way to work. We have come a long way since those days.

Manufacturing has long suffered from what I call a "3D depression"—a perception that the industry is dirty, dangerous, and demeaning. Given its early history, manufacturers have a lot to live down that hurts them today. Manufacturing cannot return to some imagined glorious past; the real issue is what it must become.

Our definition of manufacturing is evolving. It now means dealing with materials, concerns about energy and the environment, and emphasizing local manufacturing. Instead of making something and shipping it, we may send the recipe to a plant in another location and have the product made there. This is happening today with agile manufacturers and mass customization.

We are moving toward a more customized way of making things. It is not like going back to the craft era, because of the technical nature of manufacturing in many sectors. Nonetheless, I expect we are moving toward making items on a smaller scale. My grandson works for a nuclear pharmacy and creates drugs unique to the individual for whom they are prescribed. That harkens back to an older way of doing things, a more personalized approach.

Nanotechnology offers the promise of superior materials. In pharmaceutical manufacturing, for example, people are working on nanobots that deliver a molecular dose of a drug to an exact spot in a patient's body. This is the kind of thing that will undermine the factory model of manufacturing. However, the technological side of manufacturing is pretty simple compared to the business side.

Manufacturers are having a difficult time filling positions. This is not new. It has been this way for a while. Technical skill is important, of course. But manufacturers want workers to participate in making the process better. They want workers who can think. Do you have a problem? How do you know you have a problem? You do not unless you see a condition that is different from how you realize it should be—and that requires imagination and experience.

In today's manufacturing facilities, no one is going to solve a problem for you. You have got to see it and figure it out. When we talk about process improvement in manufacturing—quality, Six Sigma, lean manufacturing, whatever it is called—most of it comes down to problem solving. There are techniques to use, but an awful lot of it is learning to see, to observe, to codify what you see, and to base your logic on facts. This is a discipline, and it is not easy to acquire.

To learn how to think, you have got to be exposed to the issues and be willing to dig in. A good deal of the work of making things is learning how to do it. Then it is a matter of practice and having a mentor. I could tell you how to swim in less than a half an hour, maybe even in five minutes. But you cannot learn to swim without swimming.

The stereotype of manufacturing goes back to the assembly line—making the Model T, putting lug nuts on a wheel. For the most part that era has passed. This is not your grandfather's skill set. To succeed in manufacturing today, it takes someone who is fascinated by the process, someone who is willing to learn. When we talk about needing people with skills for manufacturing jobs, what we mean are the skills to learn and to ask questions. Manufacturing is not a career for those who want to check their brains at the door.

Like any occupation, working in manufacturing should bring satisfaction. I do not know a single person over the age of 60 who, when asked about satisfaction over his or her lifetime, answered that they were ultimately satisfied by money or something they owned. Each mentioned something they had done—champion athlete, best bowler in the league, top machinist in the plant. This accomplishment is what sets them apart.

Manufacturing is vital to the U.S. economy. Someone has to make the food we eat and the stuff we use. It is quite true that we are well below the historical peak of manufacturing employment. I do not think it ever exceeded 21 million people, and that was in 1979. We are at a little over half that now, and employment will probably decline further. We are sending manufacturing capacity elsewhere via offshoring. But the other big reason we are not at peak employment is improvements in productivity. For the last 20 to 30 years, manufacturers have been improving productivity by 2 to 3 percent per year. So, unless the manufacturer makes more product, increased productivity leads to fewer employees. We no longer need hordes of people, just a few that are exceptionally well trained.

Today it seems that a lot of manufacturing is about having something to sell. A lot of lower-skilled workers mass-produce items like toys and tchotchkes. Why? What is the logic of making things just to make them? If the only objective is to crank out more stuff and keep the machines moving, we need to ask some bigger questions. Do we need it? What is quality? Is this a job worth having?

As you pursue your manufacturing career, ask yourself these questions and many others. Think about what is important to you and what interests you. Challenge yourself to learn new things and improve your skills. Manufacturing is at the forefront of innovation, research and development, and technological change. We need smart, well-trained workers who want to be part of this ongoing transformation. Manufacturers are looking for people to do something they love and get paid for it. It does not get much better than that.

—Robert W. "Doc" Hall, Ph.D.
PROFESSOR EMERITUS, DEPARTMENT OF OPERATIONS AND DECISION TECHNOLOGIES, KELLEY SCHOOL OF BUSINESS, INDIANA UNIVERSITY

Acknowledgments

My sincere thanks to:

The librarians at the Copley and Kirstein Business branches of the Boston Public Library, who provided several important books, documents, and insights that guided the research for this book.

Fabien LaPointe, Wendy Whitaker, Kevin Calhoun, John O'Connor, and Kelly Robinson for rallying to help me pin down the finer points of job searching and résumé writing.

Robert W. "Doc" Hall, Dick Alexander, Bert Wellens, Al Weatherhead, Jordan Gibennus, Will Shanley, and Lauren Cirigliano for interviews, expertise, and some really great conversations.

Jeff Galas, for making my writing look good.

Karen Stevens, who steered me toward this project and encouraged me along the way.

And for all my family and friends, for their generosity, encouragement, and friendship. And for understanding when I couldn't come out and play.

Introduction

The manufacturing industry has an interesting story to tell. It is vital to many other industries, to the entire U.S. economy, and to our trade relationships with other countries. There will always be manufacturing and manufacturing jobs in this country. There will always be a need for qualified and skilled labor to keep production lines moving and make the products we use every day. Let this book be your guide to this important and fascinating industry.

This book is a fact-packed overview of the manufacturing industry. It will tell you everything you need to know to sound like a pro your first day on the job: What shaped the industry we see today, where it is going in the next few years, what people do within and across departments, how to advance your career and take advantage of the opportunities that are out there, and how to make sense of industry jargon.

The underlying theme of the book is the *cri de coeur* from manufacturers: They are desperate to find skilled employees to help them take advantage of the technologies the 21st century has to offer.

How to Use This Book

The Foreword provides insight from Dr. Robert W. "Doc" Hall, an industry veteran who has seen just about every type of manufacturing process, in almost every type of economy. A skilled educator and industry leader, he reminds readers of the simple joy of doing what you enjoy doing. Could that be a career in manufacturing?

Chapter 1 provides an overview of the industry's history and why it looks the way it does today. One way of looking at the story is that this country got its start because of supply chain issues and trade protectionism. So it is not surprising that the manufacturing industry continued to play a key role in much of our history, and in the creation of the stereotypical American entrepreneurial spirit. This chapter also takes a look at the industry structure. Manufacturing is complex and has many different sectors that operate in very different ways. Toy manufacturers, pharmaceutical companies, makers of computer hardware, and dairy product producers do not seem to have much in common other than the fact that they all make things to sell to others. Chapter 1 also contains an interview with Dick

Alexander, who has been in the industry for 45 years, in which he gives us his insight about the industry's history and what it means for us today.

Chapter 2 takes a look at the factors impacting the industry right now. Technological advances have drastically improved processes, productivity, and profits, and have entirely altered the way some companies do business. Nanotechnology and green manufacturing are the current buzzwords in the industry. They are both having a tremendous impact on manufacturing processes, and their importance is growing. Environmental engineering guru Bert Wellens provides insight into what it really means to be green in this business, and why it is so important. To give you an idea of the industry landscape, this chapter also discusses important industry players, such as government organizations that play a role in many aspects of the industry, the organizations and events that will help you network with your colleagues and keep abreast of changes in the field, and the top companies in each sector.

Chapter 3 provides you with a list of jobs within the industry. The jobs are organized by how the responsibilities break out in a typical manufacturing establishment, roughly in order from product development to manufacturing and distribution: design and development; production and quality assurance; inventory and distribution; health, safety, and environment; installation, maintenance, and repair; administration and management; and engineering jobs, which may fall into any of those categories. The job descriptions include information about the education and experience needed for each job, what an employee with that title will be doing with his or her day, and what to expect in terms of advancement opportunities.

Chapter 4 gives you tips for succeeding in a manufacturing career. To do well in a manufacturing job you will need to set goals and have a plan, get up to speed with the industry through formal education and networking, challenge yourself, and learn from your mistakes. Looking for work in the field is straightforward as well. Network, search for a job opening, then ace the interview. In terms of searching for a job opening, there are some manufacturing-specific career sites for you to peruse, as well as general job search sites that list jobs in most manufacturing sectors. There are also resources to help you learn how to network and how to ace an interview. Al Weatherhead, author of the book *The Power of Adversity: Tough Times Can Make You Stronger, Wiser, and Better* shares wisdom about success that he has gained during his 60 years in manufacturing.

Chapter 5 is a glossary of industry terms. Many are general terms common to most businesses or processes, including business organization and performance terminology. Other words or phrases are specific to manufacturing or distribution, such as shipping and inventory management terms. Other entries call out specific government organizations that play a vital role in the industry or a particular sector.

Chapter 6 provides resources to help you learn more about the industry in general or a specific sector. There are descriptions of industry associations and guidance on how to identify other organizations that may be useful to you. There is a brief discussion about labor unions and a list of some of the larger ones, and a section offering advice on getting certified and finding a certification authority. There is also detailed information about searching for an educational program, and some resources to help you identify a two- or four-year college, a career or vocational school, or an appropriate apprenticeship program. In addition there is a listing of some key industry magazines. There are a tremendous number of trade magazines in each manufacturing sector, so there is also some advice about where to look to find a more complete listing. (Hint: It involves your local library.) Chapter 6 also includes a list of some interesting recent books about the industry. Use this as a starting point to read about some industry titans and whet your appetite for more.

Researching and Writing This Book

Because manufacturing is such a broad industry, it is a challenge to find comprehensive information about it, or to gather information about its individual sectors without getting overwhelmed. To help curious readers find more information about the industry, a brief discussion of how this book was researched follows.

The government was a great help in this regard. The Bureau of Labor Statistics is an invaluable source for industry information. There are all sorts of statistics and resources on the bureau's Web site. Two of the most useful are *The Occupational Outlook Handbook (OOH)* and *The Career Guide to Industries* (CGI). The OOH provides detailed descriptions of many different occupations, along with the training or education needed, the working conditions and job responsibilities, earnings forecasts and current earnings data, and the outlook for the future of the job. The CGI provided overviews of several industry sectors, and includes typical occupations and links to further resources. Both of these sources are a starting point for any search for information about occupations or employment.

Government sites were also helpful for other aspects of the research—especially information regarding export and import requirements; international trade issues and trade treaties; employment issues like apprenticeships and occupational safety; career education resources; information specific to sectors like food, agriculture, and nanotechnology; and even the occasional industry glossary. The Career Voyages Web site also provided valuable information about in-demand careers and the educational resources required for some of them.

The Web site of the National Association of Manufacturing had helpful information, as well. The white paper *Keeping America Competitive: How a Talent Shortage Threatens U.S. Manufacturing* provided valuable insight, including industry statistics and background information on the current state of employment in the industry and how employers are looking to resolve the situation. In addition, their Web sites for the career-oriented Dream It. Do It campaign provided useful information about manufacturing careers and individual jobs.

The Web sites of the many other associations and organizations listed in this book were helpful, too. They provided many useful nuggets of information about things like the structure of the industry or of a particular sector, insights into some occupations, and helped form a more complete picture of the very complex structure of the industry. The goal of this book is to help you navigate through the complex world of manufacturing, figure out the right career path, and get your dream job. And the time to start is right now.

Chapter 1

Industry History

Manufacturing has a long and storied history. After all, it is the practice of making things like garments, tools, and food—and humans have been doing that for a very long time. Manufacturing is a very important industry. Look around. Unless you are a master craftsperson, you did not make anything in the room you are in right now. Most likely, someone in a factory somewhere did that for you.

Early Days

Early manufacturing was not the industry we know today. In its most primitive form, manufacturing was the making of simple tools or the milling of grain with tools like rubbing stones or a mortar and pestle. Individuals did the work for their families or tribes, and advancements and improvements to existing processes or tools were very slow. As European civilization moved out of the wilderness in the 10th century, our current way of life began to emerge. People moved closer to each other and formed communities. The economy was largely based on agriculture. The tools people used were made by hand, one at a time, usually by the person who ended up using them. As these societies grew and became more interconnected, people started to produce tools and goods to sell to others.

These craftspeople made things with their own hands, usually in their own homes, and traveled to towns and villages to sell their goods. To help control trade for the items they made, craftspeople in fields such as weaving and metalworking created guilds and professional organizations to set prices and to restrict who could enter the field. They also set standards for the types of training or apprenticeships that were required. These organizations held monopolies—exclusive control—in their industries. As populations increased in the cities, the basis of the European economy changed from agriculture to trade. Goods were still made by hand, but trade routes, improved transportation, merchant fairs, and port cities created broader markets for them.

A major leap forward in European manufacturing was the invention of moveable and reusable type in 1400s. Not only was this a boon for communications, it was the beginning of the printing industry and the start of the modern manufacturing age—machines assisting with repetitive tasks. Another major leap forward for manufacturing happened in the 16th and 17th centuries—European people organized themselves into nation-states, which led to feelings of nationalism and then to laws protecting each nation's trade.

The age of colonialism has at its roots the manufacturing supply chain. Nations colonized lands that grew crops they wanted or had raw materials they needed for manufacturing items back home. Colonies also provided new markets in which to sell manufactured goods. This is the case with the British colonization of North America. Britain viewed the colonies primarily as producers of raw materials like iron ore and cotton and as a market for their finished goods.

Although the British saw the American colonies as links in their industrial supply chain, some key developments in manufacturing benefitted the colonists. The first sawmill was built in Maine in 1623, the first blast furnace was built in Massachusetts in 1645, and

Fast Facts

Key factors in bringing the industrial revolution to America:

- Abundance of natural resources
- Growth of the iron, machine tools, and textiles industries
- Improvements in transportation infrastructure
- Encouragement of invention and entrepreneurship
- Changing management structures
- Increased population who could act as both labor and consumer
- Improvements in communications
- Growth of wholesalers and commodities exchanges

the first paper mill in the colonies was built in Philadelphia in 1690. Because the colonists were so industrious, the British began to feel threatened by American manufacturing. They began passing laws to protect British manufacturers by forbidding the colonists (and people from other countries) from buying or selling certain items. This trade protectionism—shielding the domestic manufacturing industry by imposing taxes and a limitation on imports from colonies or other countries—was a major force behind the colonists' rebellion against British rule.

The 18th Century

As the British were pursuing their colonial aspirations in North America and beyond, the industrial revolution raged back home. Many significant manufacturing advancements can be traced to England at this time, especially in the textile industry. Inventions such as the flying shuttle and the machine loom—both important in producing cotton textiles—led the way to mechanizing processes in other industries. The development of steam power to run the textile machines changed the way factories worked.

To protect their own industries, England discouraged the export of manufacturing machinery and knowledge. Parliament passed laws prohibiting the export of plans for British textile machinery and the emigration of workers who knew about the machinery. In part because of this, the development of mass production technologies and the factory system were slow to catch on in America.

Then came Oliver Evans, who was born in Delaware and started his career in textiles. In the late 1780s outside of Philadelphia, he created a factory with a system of belts, buckets, hoppers, and rakes to fully automate the milling of flour. He also wrote a book about it: *The Young Mill-Wright and Millers Guide*. Although at first not widely accepted, his machines, along with his invention of a high-powered steam engine to power them, multiplied output. Even with Evans' success in flour mills, much of the story of the early U.S. manufacturing industry is about the textile industry, and much of that story is about New England and the Northeast, in part due to the region's many rivers and access to cheap water power to run machinery.

Despite the tenacity with which the British held onto their technologies and designs, there were a few key leaks. In the first well-known case of industrial espionage, Samuel Slater spent years as an apprentice in a textile mill in England, where he learned every part of the process and the machinery. He disguised himself to emigrate from England and came to Providence, Rhode Island, in 1791, where he set up a water-powered spinning machine—the first of its kind in America. He then took the forward-thinking step of opening the factory doors to anyone who wanted to see how it worked, and he encouraged people to copy the designs and the processes. This was an important step in bringing the industrial revolution to the United States.

At this point, Americans still looked to England for many of their products—simply because they were better made than local goods, or, as in the case of herbs or pharmaceutical plant preparations, the manufacturing processes were better understood by the British. Even with the advancements in the textile industry, household manufacturing was still the primary method of manufacturing goods in the United States. Tailors, weavers, cobblers, candle makers, and carpenters worked from home and moved around to meet customers. However, most of the goods were of low quality. As cities and towns grew, traveling traders distributed goods to consumers through general stores, where the domestic goods competed with finished goods imported from abroad.

In addition to developments in the textile industry, clock making had a profound effect on the course of manufacturing. Clock making required precision tools that needed to be correct to within a fraction of an inch. The machining skills required to create those tools were then applied to industries with similar needs, especially those that used complicated gear mechanisms. In turn, the clock making industry owed much of its manufacturing success to the concept of interchangeable parts, an idea introduced by Eli Whitney.

The Early 19th Century

By 1800 the idea of mass production had taken hold. Eli Whitney, the Massachusetts-born inventor of the cotton gin (1784), was convinced that uniform and interchangeable parts were the key to successful manufacturing. He created a system of mass producing muskets for the army using interchangeable parts. Until that time, skilled gunsmiths made muskets by hand. Whitney created metal molds, with exact measurements and precision gauges, for each part of the gun. This made the process more efficient and altered his labor needs. He could use metalworkers instead of skilled gunsmiths. His system of standardizing both the making of parts and the process was a turning point for the development of factories in this country. Whitney, like Slater before him, was willing to share his ideas with anyone.

Francis Cabot Lowell was a merchant and partner in the Boston Manufacturing Company. Also like Slater, he memorized the designs of spinning machines and power looms and used that knowledge to build the company's textile plant in Waltham, Massachusetts, in 1814, putting the spinning and weaving processes in the same factory. That plant is considered the first modern, large-scale integrated corporate manufacturing plant.

Nearly anyone with an idea and a plan could build a factory and become a manufacturer—there were few legal or social barriers to creating or improving on inventions or processes. There were no guilds or professional organizations setting standards or creating requirements for entry into an industry, and there was not an entrenched class structure to get in the way of someone with an entrepreneurial spirit. Because the constitution had removed internal trade restrictions, the market was open to anyone who wanted to buy or sell something.

The early 1800s was a rich time for developments in business. In the United States, individual states were responsible for companies residing within their borders. Initially, states were reluctant to allow companies to incorporate—the idea of limiting the liability of those involved in the company did not fit with the accepted concept of personal responsibility. But soon that practice changed, and states began to pass bills setting up rules of incorporation. Some states actively courted companies, as they saw the benefits of local industry, such as tax revenue and jobs for citizens.

The War of 1812 was a windfall for American manufacturing. Both productivity and profits increased for manufacturers who made things for the war department, and for those that continued to operate during the war. Because of increased pressures, only companies with solid business structures were able to meet wartime demands. Those were the companies that flourished, causing manufacturers to begin to pay attention to business and financial operations as well as production processes.

Supply chain and distribution rose in importance at this time as well, with transportation and infrastructure playing a key role. Until the early 1800s, roads in the United States were not very good. Many were privately owned and cost money to travel on—transporting items was time consuming, difficult, and expensive. Around this time, people started to improve existing roads and to build public ones. Since transporting goods with a horse and wagon was not always practical, people began to dig canals to transport goods. The Erie Canal, for example, was completed in 1825. Then, in 1826, the first commercial railway was built in Massachusetts—horses powered a train that was used to haul granite a few miles from Quincy to Boston, to build the Bunker Hill monument.

The Industrial Revolution

The industrial revolution fully arrived in the United States in the mid-1800s, starting in New England and the Northeast and slowly making its way to the rest of the country. Household manufacturing started to decline around 1815, but it was not until the 1850s that the tide turned and factories produced more goods overall.

Many industry sectors began to thrive at this time, including the food manufacturing business. In the United States, food-related businesses began to produce crackers, bread, and candy; refine sugar and make starch; import and sell food; and engage in activities like large-scale commercial fishing. There were improvements to the processing and storage of food as well. Patents were issued for all sorts of devices, including an artificial freezer and an ice cream maker. The screw top glass jar and a method to evaporate and store milk unrefrigerated were invented around this time, as well.

The improvement in transportation as a result of the development of railways drove the industrial revolution in the United States. Hundreds of miles of railroad track were laid in the 1820s and 1830s. In 1829, the first steam-powered locomotives were built, becoming the standard power source for train engines until the early 20th century, when the internal combustion locomotive was introduced. Early railroad activity was primarily in the northeast, but the technology slowly spread to the south and west. In 1869, the intercontinental railroad was completed, crossing the entire continent and opening up the opportunity to sell goods and do business on a national scale.

Similar to the War of 1812, the Civil War had a profound effect on American manufacturing. The union government needed equipment, clothing, medicine, and other supplies, which stimulated productivity in all manufacturing sectors, in both factories and home-based manufacturing operations. Increased demand for medicines encouraged large-scale production in the pharmaceutical industry for the first time, laying the foundation for consolidation and standardization in the industry. In other industries, pressures to produce helped spawn new technologies and new methods to keep up with demand.

However, not all industries prospered. The interconnectedness and importance of a steady, uninterrupted supply chain became clear as a result of the war. Textile industries, which were largely based in the Northeast, suffered during the war because of the lack of raw materials from the cotton-producing South.

After the war ended in 1865 the trend toward industrialization picked up speed. So did the burgeoning movement to protect workers. As manufacturing became more mechanized and machines replaced human labor, fewer skilled workers were needed. While financial profit had been an important motive for a few hundred years, business structure was changing so that in some cases profit was now the only measurement that mattered. As factories hoped to increase profits by reducing labor costs, they hired workers with little training or skill. In some industries, this led to factories hiring women, children, and immigrants to do the work as cheaply as possible.

Strikes like the Trainman's Union strike of 1877 helped propagate the idea that collective action was the only way for workers to protect their rights. As part of this trend toward organization as a way to protect workers' rights, the American Federation of Labor was founded in 1886 as a safe haven for craft union workers. The organization fought for higher wages, shorter working hours, and improved working conditions. Labor protection remained a strong force in manufacturing long after this time.

By the end of the 19th century, Americans began to realize the crucial role manufacturing played in the overall economy. Until this time, states had strict laws regarding the incorporation of companies. To protect a state's interests, companies incorporated there had to be located only in that state. In the 1880s, New Jersey changed its incorporation laws so that a company based in that state could own and manage property anywhere in the country. It was the first state to take this revolutionary step. It changed the nature of manufacturing and business: it created the basis for the first interstate holding companies, like United States Steel, one of the most famous of the time. Some of the holding companies were individual companies operating on a large scale. Others were created as management contrivances so owners could possess several operating companies and improve profits. For some owners, the type of companies they owned was not important. In many cases these large corporations, including manufacturing establishments, came about as a result of mergers, a new trend in the 1880s.

Managers and business owners looked to mergers as a way to create monopolies to allow them to control prices and prevent competition in the industry. A popular management structure for overseeing these behemoths was a board of trustees—individuals with little or no operational responsibilities, whose only job was to help the company turn a profit. This was the beginning of the business structure known as a trust. Price and competition pressures caused by trusts resulted in the beginning of the antitrust movement and stronger government involvement in the business of business. In 1890, Congress passed the Sherman Antitrust Act, which made it illegal to form a trust or business combination with the purpose of restraining trade or commerce.

Everyone Knows

The North American Industry Classification System (NAICS) was designed in cooperation with Mexico and Canada in 1997 to replace the Standard Industrial Classification (SIC) system, a U.S.-centric system. NAICS groups establishments based on the primary activities they are engaged in. "Establishments that do similar things in similar ways are classified together."

Sources:
U.S. Census Bureau:
http://www.census.gov/eos/www/naics
U.S. Bureau of Labor Statistics:
http://www.bls.gov/bls/naics.htm

Around this time key developments in power were spurring growth in manufacturing. Hydroelectric power was the next big thing in 1895. Power generated this way could travel up to 500 miles, and manufacturing plants no longer needed to be near a river to take advantage of it. In 1896, George Westinghouse got the patent rights to steam turbine generators—which were modeled on an English version—and steam-generating plants were introduced in the United States, providing manufacturers with an inexpensive energy source. These changes in power generation, distribution, and use had huge implications for the manufacturing sector—they allowed factories to power equipment, automate their processes, and increase mechanization.

For many businesses, this power surge meant a new scale to their production on one end and to the sales of their products on the other end. This had special significance for manufacturers who sold their goods directly to consumers, such as apparel makers and food producers. Now they were responsible for more parts of the process. No longer able to simply produce goods, these manufacturers needed to know how to market, sell, and distribute their products. Only companies that succeeded on all fronts succeeded as going concerns.

This rise in mass production helped give rise to the modern advertising age. Ads had been around for a while, but were becoming more sophisticated and targeted. The advertising industry grew out of this time, with professionals dedicated to creating recognizable brands, selling products through national campaigns, and working to differentiate their products from their competitors.

The Early 20th Century

As the 20th century dawned, the manufacturing industry was transformed by Henry Ford's 1903 invention of continuous flow manufacturing: the assembly line. Until this time, in most factories and manufacturing plants, each worker assembled the entire product, one at a time. Ford introduced the idea that the product would move from station to station, worker to worker, who would each be responsible for just one part of the process. This improved efficiency and enabled Ford's factory, and later many others, to increase production. In 1912 Clarence Avery conducted time and motion studies, speeding up and improving the assembly line process.

Around this time the federal government started to be more of a factor in business. In 1906 the Food and Drug Administration was founded to oversee the food and pharmaceutical industries. The Federal Trade Commission was founded in 1914 with the goal of preventing unfair competitive practices. In 1918, the American National Standards Institute was created to study production methods and set standards for manufacturing processes. During World War I, the War Industries Board was created to sort through the production demands of the military, coordinate wartime production, create new manufacturing facilities if necessary, convert existing plants to war production, and allocate raw materials to establishments manufacturing goods for the war effort.

By the end of World War I, manufacturers were able to take the efficiencies and skills they learned and refocus on domestic needs and products. General Motors took two revolutionary steps around this time. The first was creating a product for every price range, which opened up the market considerably, in this case for cars. The second step was to update its products every few years. This created a built-in obsolescence and, thus, the need to purchase a new product along with a burgeoning consumer desire for the next new thing. By the time World War II erupted, the U.S. economy was global and industrial.

After World War I, the chemical industry in the United States thrived. Until that time, European companies dominated the organic chemical industry and items like dyes were imported as needed. Because of the war, that trade stopped and U.S. industry grew in areas such as petroleum refining and processing. By the start of World War II, the United States was dominant in making fibers, plastics, and other organic chemical products.

Despite the Great Depression, the 1930s saw improvements to the highway system, a new consistency in supplies of raw materials in industries like steel and fabricated metals, and an increase in automated machinery in factories. The National Industrial Recovery Act played a big part in manufacturing around this time. Intended to restructure industries to be more efficient, it included limitations on production, product standardization, and the use of labor. The government's goal was to stimulate recovery from the Depression, but the act was not popular. Among other things, it artificially raised both prices and wages and reduced manufacturers' output with a quota system. Trade protectionism reared its head at this time, too. A "buy American" philosophy tried to coerce businesses to use American raw materials and suppliers.

By the start of World War II, aircraft manufacturing was a huge industry in the United States and the war was cause for more growth. Factories built planes for Britain and France, and then for the U.S. military. As in previous wars, the demand caused by war needs led to innovations in production techniques. One major development was the practice of working more closely with subcontractors and suppliers to coordinate production. In addition, automobile plants were converted to build airplanes and tanks, and the steel industry in the United States was at full capacity for the first time.

Post–World War II

After the war, manufacturers turned to scientific research to develop new products or new applications for existing products. This was the beginning of the modern idea of research and development (R&D).

Some companies, such as Rand, were created solely to think about these abstract and theoretical concepts. R&D became common for companies in the chemical, metals, aircraft, and electronics industries, and in industries that contracted with the military. These companies produced new products, created an administrative structure to incorporate the new ideas, and managed diversified processes and operations. Around this time, the need for standardization in manufacturing processes became apparent. In 1947 the International Organization for Standardization was formed in Switzerland to create global standards for all parts of the manufacturing process, including design, manufacturing, inspection, packaging, and quality control.

The postwar period also saw the growth of paper products, plastics, and other industries closely linked with housing or power, as new home construction boomed after the war. Demand for cars and gasoline increased as well, stimulating chemical manufacturing. This was also the time of a great leap forward in pharmaceutical manufacturing. James Watson and Francis Crick discovered the structure of DNA, opening the door for manufacturers to eventually create products tailored to people with certain genes, and leading the way for the advances that nanotechnologies will bring to the practice of curing disease.

The development and growth of the computer industry was also a postwar phenomenon. In 1948, the mathematician Claude Shannon wrote a paper illustrating how any type of information could be quantified and reduced to numerical terms. Once it was realized that information could be handled by machines, the nature of manufacturing changed—along with the world. ENIAC, the world's first electronic digital computer, was introduced in 1946, ushering in the computer age. By the early 1950s, International Business Machines, a company that started in the 1880s manufacturing tabulating and sorting machines, improved computers with developments like random access memory and magnetic storage. These inventions made computers more accessible, and they started to become more critical to businesses. Now machines could replace human labor and human knowledge, which was a threat to the livelihood of workers of all kinds. The more streamlined and definable a task was, the greater the chance it could be automated—and that someone would be out of a job. This was, in fact, the dawn of the knowledge-based economy. Around this time, the number of service workers in the United States started to gain on the number of production workers.

Best Practice

ISO 9000 The family of standards for ensuring quality of goods and services in supplier-customer relations. Companies that meet these standards meet customer's quality requirements, applicable regulatory requirements, and work for continual performance improvement.

ISO 14000 The family of standards for addressing environmental management issues. Companies that meet these standards minimize harmful environmental effects caused by their activities, and continually improve their environmental performance.

Source: ISO (International Organization for Standardization)
http://www.iso.org

By the 1960s, mergers and acquisitions were again an important force in business. Manufacturers often sought to acquire firms that produced different products or were responsible for a different part of the supply chain. A business might own or be part of an establishment that had no relation to its core business. The importance of this was not universally agreed on. Those who viewed it positively saw the trend as protecting manufacturers from fluctuations in demand for their products. Those who viewed it negatively saw it as diluting a company's focus and threatening product quality.

Electronics manufacturers thrived in this environment. Advances in production and design improved costs and efficiencies, and opened the way for advances like integrated circuits. Companies sprung up to satisfy the new desire among businesses for computing technology. While price competition was always a factor in manufacturing, it now became a huge driver for those in the electronics or high-technology industries. In these industries, some of the production processes were quite labor intensive. The quest for cheap labor sources to keep the product cost down prompted companies to start looking for less expensive labor abroad. Raw materials and supplies had often crossed oceans and borders to play a role in U.S. manufacturing. Just as often, completed products recrossed those same borders and oceans to be sold. This was different, though. It was the first time U.S. manufacturers looked to foreign countries as places to open factories or to contract with local manufacturers to produce their finished products.

As the decade turned and manufacturers struggled with the new operational realities, the two big issues for all U.S. businesses were the environment and global competition. The Environmental Protection Agency was established in 1970 and immediately started to impact industry. New laws seriously affected the automobile and mining industries as water and air quality issues moved into the consciousness of both the government and American consumers.

International competition hit U.S. shores hard. Many U.S. manufacturers did not see the global picture. They had a firm belief in American superiority and did not perceive foreign manufacturers as competition. As a result, there was little investment in new technologies, and many U.S. manufacturers lost out to overseas companies that did make those investments.

Japan, for example, took the lead in steel production in the 1970s, as U.S. steel companies did not invest in cost-saving production technologies. The automobile industry lost out, too, in part because of the oil troubles in 1973. Japan was already making smaller and more fuel-efficient cars and was poised to take advantage of the situation. The newly invented practice of just-in-time manufacturing, supplying parts to the assembly line only when needed, contributed to the efficiency of Japanese carmakers. U.S. products could not compete and lost market share.

As the 1980s arrived, large-scale consolidation was again a theme in business. Amidst this consolidation, manufacturing lost its status as the largest sector of the U.S. economy. In 1984 the service sector surpassed it for the first time. Although the missteps in understanding global competition played a role, this shift was not so much caused by a contraction in manufacturing as a blossoming of service businesses.

In the 1990s, advances in electronics and communications technologies continued to streamline production methods, changing the nature of some manufacturing jobs and increasing the speed of business. The decade also ushered back in environmental concerns that changed the picture for manufacturers. The concept of global warming reignited interest in recycling, emissions control, and preventing water pollution. At the same time, U.S. manufacturers' relationships with the rest of the world were changing in formal ways.

The North American Free Trade Agreement took effect in 1994, and was designed to protect regional interests and shore up demand for manufactured goods. The World Trade Organization was founded in 1995 to ensure that trade among member nations flowed smoothly. While generally a positive force, it caused upheaval and nationalistic fervor in many countries and industries. Around this time, more U.S. companies moved factories abroad, lured by low labor costs, grants, favorable tax rates, and other incentives.

The 21st Century

As the 21st century got under way, manufacturing was a long way from its humble beginnings in the homes and hands of individuals, the advent of moveable type in the 1400s, and the development of machines to replace human labor. It was also a long way from where it was as the 20th century began. Innovations in computer technology and communications had significant impacts on manufacturing. Nanotechnology became an important trend—microscopic tolerances at the level of atoms and molecules allowed manufacturers to improve products like drugs, computers, food, textiles, and cosmetics.

Globalization was another trend that continued to have a strong impact on manufacturing. Some manufacturing jobs continued to be sent offshore, and many feared significant job loss. While some job loss was attributable to globalization, that was not the whole story of the decline in manufacturing jobs. As technology improved, labor efficiencies improved as well and manufacturers were able to extract more value out of each employee. Many manufacturers also suffered a labor shortage. As the industry came under fire for causing economic woes, people started to believe there were no manufacturing jobs left on U.S. soil. That was not—and is not—true.

Industry Scope

The manufacturing industry remains the largest exporter in the nation and is responsible for the lion's share of research and development dollars invested in the United States. It is also the basis for all other economic activity in this country, as it covers a wide range of industry sectors. According to the National Association of Manufacturers, every $1 of manufactured goods generates an additional

$1.37 of economic activity, and manufacturing businesses contribute one-third of all taxes collected by local and state governments.

The sector is typically divided in two categories based on the type of goods made: durable and non-durable. Durable goods are those that—as the name suggests—are typically long lasting, such as cars, airplanes, and refrigerators. Non-durable goods are those that typically have a shorter life span, such as food, cosmetics, and clothing. Manufacturing can also be divided in two categories based on customer base: business to consumer (B2C) and business to business (B2B). Business to consumer manufacturers produce goods for direct sale to individuals, such as clothing, food, and washing machines for one's home. Business to business manufacturers produce goods to be sold to other businesses, either as end products used by businesses or as components of other products, including computer server hardware, automobile components, and industrial washing machines for hotels.

As defined by the United States Bureau of Labor Statistics, the manufacturing industry is made up of establishments engaged in the mechanical, physical, or chemical transformation of materials, substances, or components into new products. It can be described as plants, factories, or mills that typically use power-driven machines and equipment to handle materials. It also includes establishments that transform materials or substances into new products by hand or in a worker's home, and those that sell products to the general public that are made in the location from which they are sold, such as bakeries, candy stores, and custom tailors. These businesses may process materials or may contract with other establishments to process materials for them. Both types are considered manufacturing establishments.

Manufacturing Subsectors

Manufacturing consists of many subsectors, given here in order of NAICS classification (in parentheses):

Food Manufacturing (NAICS 311)

Food manufacturing is the industry sector that transforms livestock and agricultural products into food products. These producers typically sell to wholesalers or retailers for distribution to customers, but

INTERVIEW

The U.S. Manufacturing System

Dick Alexander
Founder and chairman, Global Shop Solutions

What period in the history of manufacturing do you consider most important?

The time after World War II was key. In the 1950s and 1960s, the U.S. manufacturing industry saw great improvements in productivity. Starting back in the 1850s, the United States had a trade surplus. After the start of the war, and through the 1970s, manufacturing dominated the economy. There was a lot more research and development after the war, the economy was healthier, and there was a great hiring boom. We reached a peak of 25 million workers in manufacturing during that time. We are down to 14 million now, due to a couple of issues: Improvements in productivity and the rise of foreign manufacturing industries in countries like China, South Korea, Germany, and Japan. The former has made United States' manufacturing much more efficient, while the latter has seen the displacement of manufacturing jobs to global competitors with much lower direct costs for labor.

What has been the key development in manufacturing?

Automation. The automation of the design process helped shorten development time. The automation of machine tools enabled manufacturing plants to put out higher quality, almost impeccable, parts. In addition to improving productivity, machine tools allow manufacturers to optimize the materials they use, therefore making each piece cost less in terms of labor and materials. The automation of the process using enterprise resource software enables companies to efficiently capture everything from the time the customer calls for a quote, to the work order, to productivity on the shop floor, to shipping and receiving payment. These forms of automation have helped in every kind of manufacturing.

How has the history of manufacturing shaped the industry we see today?

By the start of World War II, manufacturing was taking place in huge plants. There might be 3,000 people working in a particular plant. Then manufacturers started breaking them down into smaller plants, finding that it was more efficient to have a plant with just 50 to 150 employees. Large manufacturing plants have too much structure and too much company-wide communication that needs to take place, and it simply made more sense to have smaller plants manufacture different parts to create the finished product. So in the late 1940s and early 1950s, companies started subcontracting work—locally, regionally, nationally, and eventually internationally. By the mid-1950s we could easily see the genesis of modern globalization in manufacturing.

Talk about the advent of the use of computers in manufacturing and what that did to the industry.
From the business side, manufacturers have been using computers as long as they have been around. First it was punch cards used for purchase orders and running the business side of things. Then it was mini-computers to run the office in the 1960s and 1970s. Starting about 1980 the big thing was no longer hardware, it was software. Packaged enterprise resource planning (ERP) software really helped manage both the business and the engineering aspects of a manufacturing company. It helped improve productivity, for example, by enabling just-in-time purchase of materials. Rather than keep items in inventory, manufacturers could order materials right before they needed them. With this kind of manufacturing philosophy, companies can be lean in their operations and reduce the number of people needed to create a product.

How has globalization shaped the manufacturing industry we see today?
Around 1990 several things happened to encourage globalization of manufacturing operations. It became more cost competitive to send things overseas, in part because of the weight structure of shipping. Exchange rates made it cost efficient to manufacture materials and products elsewhere, and other countries created favorable terms for U.S. companies to operate there. In some ways, employees are not really affected by globalization. They may create an estimate for a part, hit a button, and have it built—down the street or in China, depending on the part.

In other ways, globalization seriously affects U.S. employees. In the last eight years, we've lost about 3 million jobs to trade imbalances—jobs going overseas because it is more efficient or less expensive to manufacture parts or products outside our borders. This trade deficit—more materials coming into the United States than going out—started in 1971 and has continued through today (with the exception of 1973). There is evidence that continuing to outsource jobs overseas is antithetical to our economic growth. Restoring a balance of trade may very well help the economy, create new manufacturing jobs, and shore up the U.S. manufacturing sector.

▼

establishments that are primarily retail and make products in their location, like bakeries, are also included. Food manufacturing consists of the following types of establishments:

- Animal Food Manufacturing
- Grain and Oilseed Milling
- Sugar and Confectionery Product Manufacturing
- Fruit and Vegetable Preserving and Specialty Food Manufacturing
- Dairy Product Manufacturing
- Animal Slaughtering and Processing
- Seafood Product Preparation and Packaging
- Bakeries and Tortilla Manufacturing
- Other Food Manufacturing

Beverage and Tobacco Product Manufacturing (NAICS 312)

Beverage and tobacco product manufacturing is the industry sector that makes non-alcoholic beverages, alcoholic beverages produced by fermentation, such as wine and beer, and alcoholic beverages produced by distillation, such as rum and tequila. Ice manufacturing is included in the non-alcoholic beverage sector because it uses the same production process as water purification. The tobacco manufacturing sector includes producers of tobacco products such as cigarettes and cigars, as well as producers who re-dry and stem tobacco.

Textile Mills (NAICS 313)

Textile manufacturing is the industry sector that transforms basic fibers into products like fabric or yarn that is then manufactured into usable items like apparel, towels, and textile bags. The secondary level—manufacturing the yarn or fabric into usable goods—may be performed in the same establishment or may be classified in another sector of manufacturing. For example, manufacturers that engage only in knitting, but not the completion of the garment, are included in this sector. Manufactures that knit fabric and then produce complete garments are considered apparel manufacturers.

Textile Product Mills (NAICS 314)

Textile product mill manufacturing is the industry sector that makes all textile products other than apparel, such as sheets and towels, typically by purchasing, cutting, and sewing fabric into the end product.

Apparel Manufacturing (NAICS 315)

Apparel manufacturing is the industry sector that makes apparel products using two different processes: cut and sew—purchasing, cutting, and sewing fabric into garments; and knit, cut, and sew—establishments that first knit the fabric, then cut and sew it into garments. This sector includes a wide range of manufacturing establishments: those making ready-to-wear apparel; those making custom apparel; contractors who perform cutting or sewing operations for others; jobbers who perform entrepreneurial functions; and tailors who manufacturing custom apparel for individual clients.

Leather and Allied Product Manufacturing (NAICS 316)

Leather and allied product manufacturing is the industry sector that transforms animal hides into leather by tanning or curing, and fabricating the leather into products for final consumption. The industry also includes the manufacturing of similar non-apparel products from leather substitutes because they are made with similar processes as leather goods. These include items made with rubber, plastics, or textiles, such as rubber footwear, textile luggage, and plastic wallets.

Wood Product Manufacturing (NAICS 321)

Wood product manufacturing is the industry sector that produces wood products like lumber, veneers, wood flooring, wood containers, manufactured homes, and prefabricated wood buildings. These establishments engage in production processes including sawing, planing, shaping, laminating, and assembling of wood products. This sector includes establishments that make products from wood that has been sawed and shaped, and also establishments that purchase sawed lumber and make wood products. With the exception of sawmills and wood preservation, these establishments are grouped into industries by the specific products they manufacture.

Paper Manufacturing (NAICS 322)

Paper manufacturing is the industry sector that makes pulp, paper, and converted paper products. Often, the processes are carried out in a single establishment. Pulp manufacturing involves separating cellulose fibers in wood or used paper, and paper manufacturing involves matting those fibers into sheets. Converted paper product manufacturing involves cutting, shaping, coating, and laminating paper and other materials.

Printing and Related Support Activities (NAICS 323)

Printing and its support activities is the industry sector that prints products like newspapers, books, business cards, and other materials. The support activities, such as data imaging, plate making, and bookbinding, are an integral part of the industry.

Petroleum and Coal Products Manufacturing (NAICS 324)

Petroleum and coal products manufacturing is the industry sector based on the transformation of crude petroleum and coal into usable products. Petroleum refining—separating crude petroleum into component parts—is the dominant process in this industry sector. In addition, the sector includes establishments that further process refined petroleum and coal products, and produce final products like asphalt and petroleum lubricating oils.

Chemical Manufacturing (NAICS 325)

Chemical manufacturing is the industry sector that transforms organic and inorganic raw materials through chemical processes. This sector includes establishments that produce basic chemicals and those that further process basic chemicals to produce intermediate and end products. Chemical manufacturing consists of the following types of establishments:

- Basic Chemical Manufacturing
- Resin, Synthetic Rubber, and Artificial Synthetic Fibers and Filaments Manufacturing
- Pesticide, Fertilizer, and Other Agricultural Chemical Manufacturing
- Pharmaceutical and Medicine Manufacturing
- Paint, Coating, and Adhesive Manufacturing
- Soap, Cleaning Compound, and Toilet Preparation Manufacturing
- Other Chemical Product and Preparation Manufacturing

Plastics and Rubber Products Manufacturing (NAICS 326)

Plastics and rubber products manufacturing is the industry sector that produces goods by processing plastics and raw rubber. Plastics and rubber are combined because plastics are often used as a substitute for rubber. However, this sector is generally restricted to establishments that produce products made of just one material—just plastic or just rubber.

Nonmetallic Mineral Product Manufacturing (NAICS 327)

Nonmetallic mineral product manufacturing is the industry sector that transforms mined or quarried nonmetallic minerals, such as sand, gravel, stone, and clay into products for intermediate or final consumption. Processes in this industry include grinding, mixing, cutting, shaping, and honing. Heat is often used and chemicals are often mixed to change the composition, purity, and chemical properties of a product. Nonmetallic mineral product manufacturing consists of the following types of establishments:

- Clay Product and Refractory Manufacturing
- Glass and Glass Product Manufacturing
- Cement and Concrete Product Manufacturing
- Lime and Gypsum Product Manufacturing
- Other Nonmetallic Mineral Product Manufacturing

Primary Metal Manufacturing (NAICS 331)

Primary metal manufacturing is the industry sector that smelts or refines ferrous and nonferrous metals from ore, pig, or scrap, using electrometallurgical and other techniques. Establishments in this sector also manufacture metal alloys and superalloys by introducing chemical elements to pure metals. The output of smelting and refining is used to make sheet, strip, bar, rod, or wire, and to make castings and other basic metal products. Primary metal manufacturing consists of the following types of establishments:

- Iron and Steel Mills and Ferroalloy Manufacturing
- Steel Product Manufacturing from Purchased Steel
- Alumina and Aluminum Production and Processing
- Nonferrous Metal (except Aluminum) Production and Processing
- Foundries

Fabricated Metal Manufacturing (NAICS 332)

Fabricated metal manufacturing is the industry sector that transforms metal into intermediate or end products, with the exception of machinery, computers or electronics, and metal furniture. This is also the industry sector that treats metals and metal-formed products fabricated elsewhere. Processes in this industry include forging, stamping, bending, forming, and machining to shape individual pieces of metal, and other processes, such as welding and assembling, to join separate parts together. Establishments in this sector may use just one process or a combination of them. Fabricated metal manufacturing consists of the following types of establishments:

- Forging and Stamping
- Cutlery and Handtool Manufacturing
- Architectural and Structural Metals Manufacturing
- Boiler, Tank, and Shipping Container Manufacturing
- Hardware Manufacturing
- Spring and Wire Product Manufacturing
- Machine Shops; Turned Product; and Screw, Nut, and Bolt Manufacturing

- Coating, Engraving, Heat Treating, and Allied Activities
- Other Fabricated Metal Product Manufacturing

Machinery Manufacturing (NAICS 333)

Machinery manufacturing is the industry sector that creates end products that apply mechanical force, such as the application of gears and levers, to perform work. Processes in this industry include forging, stamping, bending, forming, and machining to shape individual pieces of metal, and welding and assembling to join separate parts together. These processes are similar to those used in metal fabricating establishments, but differ in that machinery manufacturing typically employs multiple metal forming processes in making the various parts of the machine, and in the complex assembly operations. Machinery manufacturing consists of the following types of establishments:

- Agriculture, Construction, and Mining Machinery Manufacturing
- Industrial Machinery Manufacturing
- Commercial and Service Industry Machinery Manufacturing
- Ventilation, Heating, Air-Conditioning, and Commercial Refrigeration Equipment Manufacturing
- Metalworking Machinery Manufacturing
- Engine, Turbine, and Power Transmission Equipment Manufacturing
- Other General Purpose Machinery Manufacturing

Computer and Electronic Product Manufacturing (NAICS 334)

Computer and electronic product manufacturing is the industry sector that manufactures computers, computer peripherals, communications equipment, and similar electronic products, as well as establishments that manufacture components for such products. The manufacturing processes for this sector are fundamentally different from the manufacturing processes of other machinery and equipment. The design and use of integrated circuits and the application of highly specialized miniaturization technologies are common elements in the production of computers and electronics. Computer and electronic product manufacturing consists of the following types of establishments:

- Computer and Peripheral Equipment Manufacturing
- Communications Equipment Manufacturing
- Audio and Video Equipment Manufacturing
- Semiconductor and Other Electronic Component Manufacturing
- Navigational, Measuring, Electromedical, and Control Instruments Manufacturing
- Manufacturing and Reproducing Magnetic and Optical Media

Electrical Equipment, Appliance, and Component Manufacturing (NAICS 335)

Electrical equipment, appliance, and component manufacturing is the industry sector that generates, distributes, and uses electrical power. Electric lighting equipment establishments produce electric lamp bulbs, lighting fixtures, and parts. Household appliance establishments produce both small and major electrical appliances and parts. Electrical equipment establishments make goods such as electric motors, generators, and transformers. Other electrical equipment and component establishments make devices for storing electrical power, like batteries, devices for transmitting electricity, like insulated wires, and wiring devices, like electrical outlets and light switches.

Transportation Equipment Manufacturing (NAICS 336)

Transportation equipment manufacturing is the industry sector that produces equipment for transporting people and goods. The manufacturing processes for this sector are similar to the manufacturing processes of other machinery and equipment, but this is a separate industry sector because of its size and significance. Processes in this industry include bending, welding, forming, machining, and assembling metal or plastic parts into components or finished products.

The assembly of components, subassemblies, and their further assembly into finished vehicles tend to be a more common process in this sector than in the machinery manufacturing sector. Transportation equipment manufacturing consists of the following types of establishments:

- Motor Vehicle Manufacturing
- Motor Vehicle Body and Trailer Manufacturing
- Motor Vehicle Parts Manufacturing
- Aerospace Product and Parts Manufacturing
- Railroad Rolling Stock Manufacturing
- Ship and Boat Building
- Other Transportation Equipment Manufacturing

Furniture and Related Product Manufacturing (NAICS 337)

Furniture and related product manufacturing is the industry sector that makes furniture and related articles such as mattresses, window blinds, cabinets, and fixtures. The processes in this industry include cutting, bending, molding, laminating, and assembly of such materials as wood, metal, glass, plastics, and rattan. The production process for furniture also includes design for both aesthetics and function, which may take place within the establishment or may be purchased from industrial designers.

Miscellaneous Manufacturing (NAICS 339)

Miscellaneous manufacturing is the industry sector that produces a wide range of products that cannot easily be classified as other types of manufacturing. This sector includes establishments as diverse as sporting or athletic goods manufacturers, toy and doll manufacturers, jewelry manufacturers, and medical equipment and supplies manufacturers.

A Brief Chronology

1440: Moveable and reusable type invented by Johannes Guttenberg.

1530: Foot driven spinning wheel invented.

1642: First calculating machine, worked by a series of wheels and ratchets, designed by Blaise Pascal in France.

1645: First American iron blast furnace in Lynn, Massachusetts.

1690s: First multiplying and dividing machine designed by Gottfried Leibniz.

1733: John Kay develops the flying shuttle for use in weaving.

1787: Fully automated flourmill designed by Oliver Evans.

1790: U.S. Patent office opens.

1791: First efficient American machine to spin cotton thread introduced by Samuel Slater.

1792: Early version of the New York Stock & Exchange Board started.

1798: Continuous paper making machine invented.

1800: Mass production, using molds and interchangeable parts, invented by Eli Whitney.

1814: First integrated textile plant in Waltham, Massachusetts, designed by Francis Cabot Lowell. First steam powered newspaper press installed.

1817: New York Stock & Exchange Board formalized.

1822: Difference engine, machine to make tabulations, designed by Charles Babbage.

1825: Erie Canal completed.

1826: First commercial railway from Quincy to Boston, Massachusetts.

1833: National road in Maryland, Virginia, and Ohio completed.

1838: Law requiring originality in patent applications enacted.

1839: Vulcanized rubber invented by Charles Goodyear.

1842: Grain elevator patented by Joseph Dart.

1844: Samuel Morse sends first Morse code message.

1846: Sewing machine patented by Elias Howe.

1849: First labor union organized, in Pennsylvania.

1851: Process to burn impurities out of steel and iron invented by William Kelly. Vernier caliper, making measurements to a thousandth of an inch possible, invented by J.R. Brown.

1855: Process to create large ingots of steel patented by Henry Bessemer.

1856: Method to evaporate and store milk in unrefrigerated cans perfected by Gail Borden.

1858: Screw top glass jar invented by John Mason.

1858: Crude oil discovered in Pennsylvania, beginning the American petroleum industry.

1862: Pasteurization invented.

1869: Transcontinental railroad completed. Cigarette mass production machine invented by James Buchanan Duke.

1875: Andrew Carnegie opens up the first integrated steel works.

1876: Telephone invented by Alexander Graham Bell.

1881: First automated buttonhole machine patented.

1886: American Federation of Labor (AFL) founded.

1895: First hydroelectric power plant completed at Niagara Falls.

1899: First telephone wires linking exchanges in different cities installed.

1901: Steam powered delivery trucks become popular. Ransom E. Olds establishes assembly line technique as a method of putting cars together.

1906: Food and Drug Administration created.

1911: Mack trucks with 7.5 ton capacity become available.

1912: Clarence Avery time and motion studies speed up assembly line process.

1913: Aluminum foil used for the first time in packaging food.

1914: Assembly line perfected by Henry Ford. Federal Trade Commission created.

1918: American National Standards Institute (ANSI) created.

1920: Sterilization of canned food begins.

1923: Continuous hot-strip rolling of steel invented.

1928: First all-electric television demonstrated.

1933: President Herbert Hoover signs the Buy American Act.

1935: National Labor Relations Board created. Plexiglas introduced.

1938: Congress of Industrial Organizations (CIO) forms as independent organization. Teflon and nylon are invented.

1946: Electrical Numerical Integrator and Computer (ENIAC), a computer 1,000 times faster than any calculating machine yet invented, completed.

1947: General Agreement on Tariffs and Trade (GATT) formed. Transistor invented.

1950: UNIVAC, the first mass-produced computer for business use, is built.

1954: Polypropylene invented. Frozen TV dinners introduced.

1955: AFL and CIO merge.

1957: First nuclear power plant goes into operation.

1958: Integrated circuit invented.

1959: Computer assisted manufacturing debuts.

1960: First commercial modem invented.

1962: Disk storage systems for computer introduced by IBM.

1963: Lithium technology invented.

1967: Semiconductor invented.

1970: Environmental Protection Agency created. Occupational Safety and Health Administration created. Just-in-time manufacturing pioneered in Japan.

1971: First e-mail sent. Soft contact lenses introduced.

1981: Personal computers launched.

1984: Service sector surpasses manufacturing as the largest sector in the American economy. Apple Macintosh launched.

1989: Virtual reality emerges.

1990: World Wide Web created.

1994: North American Free Trade Agreement takes effect.

1995: World Trade Organization formed.

Chapter 2

State of the Industry

Manufacturing is crucial to the U.S. economy. It accounts for 62 percent of research and development in this country, and is responsible for almost a third of productivity growth. In terms of job creation, the industry has the highest multiplier effect: Every $1 million of final sales supports eight manufacturing jobs and six jobs in other industries, such as services and agriculture.

It is a complex industry. U.S. owned firms mix with foreign-owned entities. Raw materials and supplies come from inside the United States and from all over the world. In some sectors, parts are built here and assembled elsewhere. Or vice versa. There is a tremendous amount of trade in raw materials, partial goods, and final products. Because of this massive movement of goods, manufacturing is tied closely to trade and to the fate of the overall economy. That means that the industry is cyclical like the economy, and that it declines when the economy contracts.

Productivity is a key component of the success of manufacturing businesses. Productivity gains resulting from automated processes are good for company profits. Yet they often lead to a restructuring of the workforce and a loss of jobs for those whose skills no longer match the needs of the company.

Because the process of making things has been around for so long and the industry is so important to the U.S. economy, it is easy to think of the industry as a stable and consistent force. Yet it is quite volatile. Because of that volatility and constant change, today's manufacturing industry faces a number of challenges—such as a shortage of labor, globalization and offshoring, rising costs for healthcare and energy, and concerns about its impact on the environment.

Manufacturing and the Economy

In school, we do not learn much about manufacturing. We are taught about Henry Ford and the development of the assembly line, and we might read Upton Sinclair's *The Jungle* or hear the depressing tale of the Triangle Shirtwaist factory fire. Unfortunately, these limited glimpses are what provide most people with their understanding of the industry: they think that the work is dark, dangerous, dirty, repetitive, low paying, and low status. The reality of manufacturing today is much different, but these images have had a strong and lasting impact on the state of the industry.

Workforce Shortage

Ask almost any manufacturer and they will tell you that they are losing workers to retirement and career changes and that they are not able to fill open positions. They will talk about projections that say the industry will need 10 million new skilled workers by the year 2020. They will tell you how difficult it is to convince young workers that the industry is high-tech, innovative, exciting, and well paying. They will talk about something that is true of almost all of corporate America—that it is difficult to find qualified employees with the appropriate technical skills.

Manufacturers will also tell you how the work ethic and expectations of younger workers are changing the way we work in all industries and economic sectors. Today's workers are mobile and apt to switch companies as a path to advancement. Gone are the days of a worker spending his or her career employed by one company, working up the career ladder. This is an adjustment for some in the manufacturing industry.

International Trade

Manufactured goods make up the bulk of international trade and the United States is still the largest exporter of goods and services in the world. But global competition is strong. From outside U.S. borders, competition comes from companies that have lower labor costs or favorable trade terms. This leads to a tremendous pressure

Fast Facts

Alphabet Soup: Trade Agreements

Global
- WTO–World Trade Organization

Regional
- APEC–Asia-Pacific Economic Cooperation
- CAFTA-DR–Dominican Republic-Central America-United States Free Trade Agreement
- FTAA–Free Trade Area of the Americas
- NAFTA–North American Free Trade Agreement
- MEFTA–Middle East Free Trade Area Initiative

Bilateral
- FTA–Free Trade Agreement
- TIFA–Trade and Investment Framework Agreement
- BIT–Bilateral Investment Treaty

Source: Office of the United States Trade Representative: http://www.ustr.gov

on U.S.-based manufacturers to reduce costs and increase productivity in order to remain competitive.

Recent economic growth can be tied to the removal of some trade barriers, in addition to increased productivity. In the ten years from 1990 to 2000, exports from the United States increased by 98 percent and increased from being 11.4 percent of world trade to 12.2 percent. Spurred by growth and international competition, U.S. manufacturers became more quality-conscious and productive.

Trade agreements play a critical role in how competitive American firms can be in the global marketplace. The federal government works to secure the best terms for the sale of products made in the United States to customers outside our borders, to keep costs of imported materials as low as possible for U.S. firms, and to stimulate manufacturing and economic growth. At the same time, governments in other countries are creating policies for the very same reason—to give their businesses the advantage.

The North American Free Trade Agreement, for example, is a combined effort of Canada, Mexico, and the United States. The idea is for these three countries to work together as trading partners in a way that benefits manufacturers and suppliers. Although it is difficult to gauge the treaty's direct effect on the U.S. labor market because of the complexity of the economy and employment, it has created some instability and jobs have been lost as a result. However, because of the new trading terms, the export of goods and materials to Canada and Mexico has created more jobs than were lost, and the net effect was an increase of jobs in the United States, although often in industries other than manufacturing.

International trade is a delicate game. Manufacturers, suppliers, and buyers across the world are connected in numerous and sometimes confusing ways. Governments must be gentle in protecting the rights and livelihoods of their businesses and residents, while acknowledging and accepting the interconnections and working to be responsible global citizens.

Globalization

If it ever did make sense to consider some manufacturing sectors uniquely American, it no longer does. Manufacturing is a global game, in some sectors more than others. Raw materials, assembly of intermediate and final products, and markets for products and materials exist everywhere.

In recent years some U.S. manufacturers have moved some of their operations offshore to cut costs and improve productivity. Because labor costs and tariffs and taxes are different the world over, it is possible to save costs by moving parts of an operation to another location, even factoring in the cost of shipping the item to various locales. Contrary to popular belief, though, not all manufacturing jobs have gone overseas and of those that have, not all have gone to China or Mexico.

It is true that some manufacturers have expanded operations to developing or low-wage countries by opening an operating division there, contracting with a third party provider, or affiliating with a local company. Yet it is also true that some manufacturers have operations or affiliates in European Union countries. In the last decade, for example, less than 20 percent of foreign direct investment of U.S. firms has gone to low-wage economies.

Globalization also means that foreign-owned firms invest here, locating operations in the United States or affiliating with U.S.-based companies. In fact, foreign firms invest in the United States in greater amounts than U.S. firms invest abroad. Whether it is a multinational corporation, a foreign-owned firm, or a domestic company, when manufacturing operations are located in the United States the net effect is the creation of jobs in this country.

U.S. Government

In 2009 the government took a hands-on approach to some manufacturing businesses, including General Motors and Chrysler. This type of direct involvement in manufacturing is unusual and was undertaken with hopes of buoying the companies, their suppliers, the industry and, by extension, the economy during a recession. Regardless of this atypical direct involvement, the government does play a large indirect role in the manufacturing industry.

In one regard, the government's role is to help U.S. manufacturers—and all businesses—participate fully and fairly in the global economy. The government creates regulations, laws, tariffs (import tariffs are collected by the U.S. government on imported goods), tax credits, and trade treaties (agreements with other governments dictating terms of import and export) to help balance imported goods and raw materials and exports of raw materials and finished goods. To encourage trade, the government has created bilateral and regional trade treaties, enabling U.S. businesses to export to and import from specific countries at beneficial rates. The World Trade Organization exists to help even out trade policies across the globe. Both approaches have their merits.

The overall role of the government in the industry is complex and the landscape of regulation and international trade is always changing. For example, Congress is charged with enacting trade regulations, including antitrust regulation to prevent collusion among U.S. companies in order to promote open and free competition. The Department of Commerce's International Trade Administration is responsible for monitoring foreign compliance with trade agreements and the United States International Trade Commission is responsible for issues like policy information, compiling trade data and making it available, and maintaining the Harmonized Tariff Schedule, which describes all trade goods and the duty rates for each.

Manufacturers are impacted by a number of laws and regulations. Depending on the industry, some government agencies have responsibility for enforcing laws. The Food and Drug Administration, for example, enforces many laws that directly affect manufacturers, including those that deal with marketing and pricing of drugs, nutrition labeling, dietary supplements, medical device safety, and animal drugs. The Environmental Protection Agency enforces laws dealing with emissions, clean air and water, and protection of the environment. The Federal Trade Commission enforces consumer protection and antitrust laws. The Federal Energy Regulatory Commission regulates interstate transportation rates and services for crude oil, petroleum, electricity, natural gas pipelines, and hydropower.

Wage and Employment Statistics

Rumors of the death of manufacturing are exaggerated. Employment is in decline, though, both in terms of the absolute number of manufacturing employees and as a percentage of the workforce. From 1982 to 2006 total employment in the economy increased, yet manufacturing as a percentage of non-agriculture employment declined from 18.5 percent to 9.1 percent during that same time. While there was a net loss in manufacturing jobs, those numbers do not tell the whole story. As some manufacturing jobs were lost, new jobs were being created, often in different sectors of the industry. The rise in total employment combined with a net loss in manufacturing represents a shift in employment from production to service sector jobs.

Part of the decline in employment in the industry is due to increased efficiency—as manufacturers automate more processes and become more efficient at others, fewer workers are needed to accomplish the same levels of productivity. Overall, this is positive for the industry, as it helps keep costs down, get products to market faster, and encourages innovation. It does, however, lead to a shift in employment—away from lower-skilled jobs to those that require more advanced or technological skills. Offshoring of jobs to foreign countries has affected the industry, but it is responsible for only a small part of the decline in manufacturing employment.

That number also does not tell the story of the desperate need many manufacturers have for skilled employees. Despite predicted decreases in most industry sectors over the next five to ten years, every sector is in need of qualified, technologically savvy employees. Among other things, attrition and retirement mean that skilled labor will always be in demand, especially for employees with computer and machine skills. The following profiles are listed in order of North American Industry Classification System (NAICS) code.

Food Manufacturing (NAICS 311)

Almost 90 percent of all food manufacturing establishments employ 100 or fewer workers, yet establishments with more than 500 employees account for approximately 35 percent of the jobs in the industry. The largest segment of the industry is animal slaughtering and processing, followed by bakeries and tortilla manufacturing. The smallest segment is seafood product preparation and packaging. In January 2009, the total number of employees was 1,470,700. Of those, 79 percent (1,171,500) were production workers. Industry unemployment was 8.1 percent in that same period. By 2016, employment in the industry is expected to grow by less than 1 percent; management occupations are projected to decrease 3.97 percent and production operations increase by 3.6 percent.

Automation in the form of computers and technologically advanced machinery is increasing productivity and limiting employment growth in most segments. However, workers who perform tasks like cutting and chopping will still be needed, as this work is difficult to automate. Additionally, as workers leave the work force there will be numerous job openings. Employment in food manufacturing tends to remain stable despite economic conditions, as people still need to eat.

In 2008, production workers averaged $14.64 per hour or $25,805 annually, with the highest earners being production managers ($23.49 per hour, $48,860 annually) and the lowest being slaughterers and meat packers ($11.18 per hour, $23,240 annually).

Beverage and Tobacco Product Manufacturing (NAICS 312)

Total employment in this industry segment in January 2009 was 194,200; 59 percent (114,600) were production workers. During that same period, unemployment in this sector was 11.9 percent. By 2016, employment in the industry is expected to decrease by 12 percent overall. Management occupations are projected to decline by 13.3 percent and production occupations by 14.9 percent.

Production workers averaged $22.76 per hour or $47,498 in 2008, with the highest earners being production managers ($44.40 per hour, $92,250 annually) and the lowest being freight, stock, and materials movers ($12.72 per hour, $26,450 annually).

Textile Mills (NAICS 313)

Most textile workers are located in California, Georgia, and North Carolina, representing 40 percent of all workers in the industry. Fabric mills are the largest industry segment, and fiber, yarn, and thread mills are the smallest. Total employment in January 2009 was 133,600, and 79 percent of those (105,400) were production workers. By 2016, overall employment in the industry is expected to decrease by 31.5 percent, management occupations are expected to decrease by 33 percent and production operations by 31 percent.

The major reason for the projected decline in jobs in the textile and apparel industries is the advancement of manufacturing technologies like robots, wider looms, and processes that do not require spinning or weaving. Trade regulations also influence employment—in 2005, the World Trade Organization lifted quotas for this sector, allowing more imports into the United States.

Production workers averaged $14 per hour or $29,114 annually in 2008, with the highest earners being production managers ($22.15 per hour, $46,060 annually) and the lowest being winding, twisting, and drawing out machine operators ($11.37 per hour, $23,650 annually).

Textile Product Mills (NAICS 314)

As in the textile mill segment, most workers are located in California, Georgia, and North Carolina. Any growth in this industry is likely to come from the industrial fabrics, carpets, and specialty yarns sectors, as these establishments are on the cutting edge of manufacturing automation and technologies. Apparel fabric mills are expected to see declining employment as manufacturers build or acquire production capabilities in countries with less expensive labor. Total employment in January 2009 was 137,400, and 78 percent (107,100) were production workers. By 2016, employment in the industry is expected to decrease by 12.4 percent, with management occupations decreasing by 14.3 percent and production operations by 11.75 percent.

Production workers averaged $13.65 per hour or $28,403 annually in 2008, with the highest earners being production managers ($21.33 per hour, $44,370 annually) and the lowest being sewing machine operators ($10.56 per hour, $21,970 annually).

Apparel Manufacturing (NAICS 315)

Like textile mills and textile product mills, apparel manufacturing is concentrated in California, Georgia, and North Carolina. Apparel manufacturing is labor intensive and difficult to automate, so labor will always be in demand and, sometimes, offshore suppliers will satisfy that demand. The largest industry segment is cut and sew apparel manufacturing and the smallest is apparel accessories.

Apparel manufacturing is particularly sensitive to price pressures. Consumers demand lower prices and competition is fierce, including from foreign producers and labor supplies. The trend in this industry segment is toward mergers in order to cut costs and remain competitive. For workers, this may mean layoffs as firms cut staff and automate to increase efficiency. In January 2009, total employment in this sector was 178,900, with production workers making up 81 percent (144,900) of the total. By 2016, employment in the industry is expected to decrease by 54 percent overall and in both management and production occupations.

Production workers averaged $12.37 per hour or $25,740 annually in 2008, with the highest earners being production managers ($19.93 per hour, $41,450 annually) and the lowest being sewing machine operators ($9.70 per hour, $20,180 annually).

Leather and Allied Product Manufacturing (NAICS 316)

In January 2009, the industry had 32,400 employees. Production workers made up 83 percent (26,900) of the total. By 2016, employment in the industry is projected to decrease overall by 46 percent, with management occupations decreasing by 47.3 percent and production occupations by 45.3 percent.

Production workers averaged $13.73 per hour or $28,554 annually in 2008, with the highest earners being production managers ($21.68 per hour, $45,090 annually) and the lowest being sewing machine operators ($10.40 per hour, $21,620 annually).

Wood Product Manufacturing (NAICS 321)

Most wood related production jobs are close to supplies of wood, with the southeastern United States dominant for furniture-related jobs. In January 2009, total employment in this sector was 403,900, 78 percent (313,500) of which were production workers. Unemployment for the same period was 11 percent. By 2016, employment in the industry is expected to decrease by 6 percent overall, with management occupations seeing a decline of 10 percent and production occupations a decline of 2.7 percent.

Production workers averaged $14.59 per hour or $30,357 annually in 2008, with the highest earners being production managers ($22.99 per hour, $47,810 annually) and the lowest being machine feeders ($11.83 per hour, $24,610 annually).

Paper Manufacturing (NAICS 322)

In January 2009 there were 427,300 total employees in the industry. Of those workers, 77 percent (330,300) were production workers. By 2016, employment in the industry is projected to decrease by 21.7 percent, with a 23.3 percent decline in management occupations and a 20.8 percent decline in production occupations.

Production workers averaged $23.18 per hour or $48,211 annually in 2008, with the highest earners being production managers ($43.92 per hour, $91,340 annually) and the lowest being industrial truck and tractor operators ($15.93 per hour, $33,130 annually).

Printing and Related Support Activities (NAICS 323)

Printing plants are widely distributed throughout the country, but specialized operations may be concentrated to particular geographies—such as financial documents in New York City. The largest industry segment is commercial lithographic printing, followed by commercial screen printing. The smallest is blankbook and looseleaf binder manufacturing. Newer printing technologies are affecting the number of operators and production workers required, as is the current crisis in the newspaper industry.

Total employment in the industry in January 2009 was 558,100; 70 percent of those employees (394,900) were production workers.

By 2016, employment in the industry is projected to decrease by 21.8 percent. Management occupations will see a decline of 24.7 percent and production occupations a decline of 20.3 percent.

Production workers averaged $18.48 per hour or $38,372 annually in 2008, with the highest earners being production managers ($26.26 per hour, $54,620 annually) and the lowest being bindery workers ($14.07 per hour, $29,270 annually).

Problem Solving

What A Union Can Do For You

SYSCO, a large food product and distribution company, purchased a food service division from Flickinger Company. Although the products they offered were similar, the business processes and operations were different. All of the Flickinger workers were required to reapply for their jobs to work with SYSCO. Not all the workers were rehired. The negotiations with the union were difficult, and some workers were upset with the union for not insisting that SYSCO use seniority as one of the criteria for rehiring workers. An agreement was reached and labor relations were basically good.

However, SYSCO used engineering work standards that are difficult to install in a food service company, and not what the former Flickinger employees were used to. There was a minimum performance standard and employees were paid based on their performance in compliance with the standards. Those who did not perform up to the standard were disciplined. That led to some challenges with the hourly workers, and SYSCO and the union tried to find an alternative. The company created a team with management and union members to discuss the issue. When it came time to negotiate a new contract, the incentive program was created, with pay increases tied to productivity increases. SYSCO also implemented new tools to help make the process easier. The union and SYSCO worked in partnership to look after the best interests of both parties.

Source: Champions //www.ilr.cornell.edu/wied/economic/championsAt Work/2000report.html, accessed June 5, 2009

Petroleum and Coal Products Manufacturing (NAICS 324)

Jobs in the petroleum industry are located in areas with petroleum deposits, including Alaska, California, Oklahoma, Louisiana, and Texas. Employment in petroleum and coal will decrease, as improved technologies enable extraction and refinement with fewer employees, although production workers will always be needed. In January 2009, there were 114,200 employees in the industry. Of that total, 61 percent (69,400) were production workers. Industry unemployment during that same period was 10.8 percent. Employment in the industry is expected to decrease by 23 percent by 2016. Management occupations are predicted to decrease by 26.8 percent, production occupations by 21.3 percent.

Production workers averaged $23.49 per hour or $48,870 annually, with the highest earners being production mangers ($33.22 per hour, $69,090 annually) and the lowest being mixing and blending machine setters, operators, and tenders ($16.67 per hour, $34,670 annually).

Chemical Manufacturing (NAICS 325)

The majority of chemical manufacturers are located near other manufacturing businesses or petroleum or natural gas production centers: California, Illinois, New Jersey, New York, Ohio, Pennsylvania, South Carolina, Tennessee, and Texas. The largest segment of the non-pharmaceutical chemical industry is basic chemical manufacturing, followed by soap, cleaning compound, and toilet preparation manufacturing. The smallest is pesticide, fertilizer, and other agricultural chemicals. Pharmaceutical manufacturing takes place primarily in California, Illinois, Indiana, New Jersey, New York, North Carolina, Pennsylvania, and Texas, with almost 90 percent of the jobs in establishments with more than 100 workers.

Total employment in January 2009 was 832,700. Of those employees, 497,700 (60 percent) were production workers. During that same period, unemployment was 8.1 percent. By 2016, employment in the industry is expected to decrease by 2.4 percent, management occupations are expected to increase by 0.5 percent, and production occupations are expected to decrease by 7 percent. In the non-pharmaceutical sector, overall employment is expected to decrease by 15.7 percent, in management occupations by 15.5 percent, and in production occupations by 16.2 percent. In the pharmaceutical and medicine manufacturing sector, however, employment is expected to increase: 23.7 percent overall, 26.5 percent in management occupations, and 21.9 percent in production occupations.

Production workers averaged $21.53 per hour or $44,792 annually in 2008, with the highest earners being chemists ($33.55 per hour, $69,780 annually) and the lowest being packaging and filling machine operators and tenders ($13.83 per hour, $28,770 annually).

Plastics and Rubber Products Manufacturing (NAICS 326)

In January 2009, the industry employed a total of 679,700 workers, 77 percent of whom (525,200) were production workers. Unemployment during that same period was 13.8 percent. By 2016, industry employment is expected to decrease by 4 percent. Management occupations are predicted to decline by 3.5 percent and production occupations by 4 percent.

Production workers averaged $14.85 per hour or $30,844 annually in 2008, with the highest earners being production managers ($23.64 per hour, $49,180 annually) and the lowest being hand packers and packagers ($10.97 per hour, $22,820 annually).

Nonmetallic Mineral Product Manufacturing (NAICS 327)

Mining for nonmetallic minerals—such as clay, stone, or gravel— is done in almost every state of the union. Demand in this sector is heavily affected by the construction industry, especially in the highways and road segment of the industry. Construction and maintenance of infrastructure like roads and bridges will drive growth in this sector. Total employment in January 2009 was 434,300. Production workers made up 80 percent (337,800) of that total. Unemployment during that same period was 9.4 percent. Overall industry employment is predicted to decline just slightly by 2016—0.1 percent. The projected decrease in management occupations is 3 percent and in production occupations, 2.6 percent.

Production workers averaged $16.65 per hour or $34,648 annually in 2008, with the highest earners being production managers ($25.05 per hour, $52,110 annually) and the lowest being laborers and hand freight, stock, and materials movers ($12.55 per hour, $26,110 annually).

Primary Metal Manufacturing (NAICS 331)

Steel manufacturing is broken into two sectors: Iron and steel mills and ferroalloy production with about 61 percent of the workers, and steel products from purchased steel with 39 percent of employees. Traditionally, the industry is located in the Midwest and east, with about 43 percent still located in Indiana, Ohio, and Pennsylvania. Almost 80 percent of all employees worked for establishments with 100 or more workers, although most of the establishments in this sector (82 percent) employ less than 100 workers.

In January 2009, the industry had a total of 409,300 employees, with 314,000 (77 percent) production workers. Unemployment during that same period was 11.5 percent. The outlook for the overall industry is a 29.6 percent reduction in employment by 2016. Management occupations are expected to decline 29.6 percent and production occupations by 26.6 percent.

Production workers averaged $18.49 per hour or $38,468 annually in 2008, with the highest earners being production managers ($26.43 per hour, $54,980 annually) and the lowest being cutting, punching, and press machine setters, operators, and tenders ($14.81 per hour, $30,810 annually).

Fabricated Metal Manufacturing (NAICS 332)

In January 2009, total employment in the industry was 1,425,300. Production workers made up 74 percent (1,053,700) of the employees. By 2016, overall employment in the industry is expected to decrease by 12.2 percent, with management occupations decreasing by 15.6 percent and production occupations decreasing by 12.2 percent. In 2008, production workers averaged $17.37 per hour or $36,130 annually, with the highest earners being production managers ($26.04 per hour, $54,170 annually) and the lowest being team assemblers ($13.34 per hour, $27,740 annually).

Machinery Manufacturing (NAICS 333)

Machinery manufacturing takes place throughout the country, but about 33 percent of all the jobs are in the Midwest: Illinois, Indiana, Michigan, Ohio, and Wisconsin. California, New York, Pennsylvania, and Texas also have significant machinery manufacturing jobs. The largest segment of the industry is agriculture, construction, and mining machinery, followed by metalworking machinery. The smallest segment is engine, turbine, and power transmission equipment. Although there is strong, yet cyclical, demand for machinery in all industries, productivity growth and imported parts will temper employment gains generated from demand alone.

In January 2009, total employment in the industry was 1,126,000, with production workers making up 64 percent of employees (715,800). Unemployment during this period was 9.2 percent. By 2016, employment in the industry is expected to decrease by 12.3 percent, with management occupations down 15.4 percent and production occupations down 12 percent.

In 2008, production workers averaged $19.54 per hour or $40,645 annually, with the highest earners being mechanical engineers ($33.38 per hour, $69,430 annually) and the lowest being team assemblers ($14.27 per hour, $29,680 annually).

Computer and Electronic Product Manufacturing (NAICS 334)

Many computer and electronic product manufacturing establishments are small, employing just one worker. However, establishments with 100 or more employees make up the bulk of the industry. The largest segment of the industry is semiconductor and other electronic component manufacturing, followed by navigational, measuring, electromedical, and control instruments. The smallest sector is audio and visual equipment manufacturing. Technology developments happen quickly, and this means that the industry is subject to severe downturns. Add in competition from imports, and it is clear that the employment in the industry can be volatile.

In January 2009, the industry employed a total of 1,212,900 workers. A little more than half (699,500) were production workers. During that same time period, unemployment was 7.9 percent. By 2016, employment in the industry is expected to decrease by 12 percent, management occupations by 12.9 percent, and production occupations by 16 percent.

In 2008, production workers averaged $32.80 per hour or $68,231 annually, with the highest earners being computer hardware engineers ($49.06 per hour, $102,040 annually) and the lowest being electrical and electronic equipment assemblers ($14.34 per hour, $29,830 annually).

Electrical Equipment, Appliance, and Component Manufacturing (NAICS 335)

Total employment in the industry was 406,100 in January 2009, with 72 percent of employees (292,800) working in production. Unemployment during that same period was 11.2 percent. Overall employment in the industry by 2016 is expected to decrease by 18.6 percent. In that same time period, management occupations are expected decrease by 17.9 percent and production occupations by 20 percent.

Production workers averaged $16.34 per hour or $33,981 annually in 2008, with the highest earners being production managers ($25.31 per hour, $52,640 annually) and the lowest being team assemblers ($14.07 per hour, $29,260 annually).

Transportation Equipment Manufacturing (NAICS 336)

Motor vehicle manufacturing is concentrated in the Illinois, Indiana, Michigan, Ohio, and Tennessee. Those states are home to 54 percent of the jobs in the industry. More than half of these establishments employ 500 or more workers. Aerospace product and parts manufacturing is concentrated in California and Washington, although there are also many manufacturers in Arizona, Connecticut, Kansas, and Texas. Most of these manufacturers are subcontractors that make parts and employ less than 100 employees. Yet 62 percent of all employees in the industry work in establishments with more than 1,000 employees.

The industry employed a total of 1,423,500 people in January 2009. Of those, 1,010,100 (71 percent) were production workers. Unemployment during that same period was 14.6 percent. Overall industry employment is expected to decrease by 6.5 percent by 2016. In that time, management occupations will likely decrease by 6 percent and production occupations by 9.5 percent. The motor vehicle parts and manufacturing segment is expected to decline further than the transportation equipment industry as a whole—down 14.3 percent overall, with management occupations declining by 13.8 percent and production occupations declining by 14.4 percent.

For the entire industry in 2008, production workers averaged $26.34 per hour or $54,794 annually, with the highest earners being aerospace engineers ($41.43 per hour, $86,160 annually) and the lowest being team assemblers ($16.07 per hour, $33,430 annually).

Furniture and Related Product Manufacturing (NAICS 337)

In January 2009, the industry employed a total of 428,600 workers. Production workers represented 75 percent (320,400) of total employees. Unemployment during this period was 14.5 percent. Overall employment in the industry is expected to decrease by 6.4 percent by 2016, with management occupations decreasing by 10.4 percent and production occupations decreasing by 5.7 percent.

In 2008, production workers averaged $15.65 per hour or $32,541 annually, with the highest earners being production managers ($23.14 per hour, $48,140 annually) and the lowest being team assemblers ($12.63 per hour, $26,260 annually).

Miscellaneous Manufacturing (NAICS 339)

It is difficult to predict the growth or decline of this market, as the establishments vary significantly—from sporting goods, to toys, to jewelry, to medical products. Each has unique influences and market demands. As a whole, this catchall sector employed 611,000 workers in January 2009. Production workers made up 66 percent (400,700) of the total. During this same period, unemployment across each of these miscellaneous industries was 10.3 percent. Overall employment in this sector is expected to decrease by 8 percent by 2016. It is predicted that management occupations will decline by 8.9 percent and production occupations by 7.9 percent.

Production workers averaged $19.07 per hour or $39,660 annually in 2008, with the highest earners being wholesale and manufacturing sales representatives for non-scientific or non-technical products ($29.76 per hour, $61,910 annually) and the lowest being team assemblers ($12.49 per hour, $25,970 annually).

Unions and Manufacturing

Union membership is declining in the manufacturing industry, as it is in the economy overall. In 2005, 13 percent of manufacturing employees were members of unions or covered by a union contract. That number decreased to 11.4 percent in 2008, slightly lower than the entire private sector workforce figure of 12 percent. That is down from the high point for the entire workforce in 1953 when 32 percent of the entire workforce were union members. The decrease is

INTERVIEW

Greening the Process

Bert Wellens
Overseer, Sustainable energy management, MWH

What is green manufacturing?
Green manufacturing is a way to manufacture a product with as limited an environmental footprint as possible. By "footprint" I mean not only energy use, but also things like raw materials, water usage, and emissions. There is no one technique or technology to enable green manufacturing. It is more of a mindset—taking one step back regularly and evaluating the process, the facilities, and the supply chain, looking for inefficiencies.

There are typically four categories where this review can make a difference: 1) Process controls, both the technical optimization and the evaluation of set points. 2) Detailed design of the manufacturing process. 3) Equipment substitution, meaning replacement of poorly performing equipment. 4) Integration—trying to find that perfect balance in your facility, such as re-using wastewater from one process to supply water for another process.

It is a challenge to know what companies and processes really are green. Is there an industry group or other certification process? If not, what should someone look for to know that a manufacturer or process is truly green?
There is not an easy answer to this question. First, green manufacturing is a combination of elements, both in the design and manufacturing processes. Many products are no longer made in a single facility, so suddenly it is the entire supply chain you are talking about. A manufacturer can make the last step of the process green, but that does not mean the final product is green.

The first priority for any manufacturer is quality. Full stop. The second is cost savings. The third should be making the process green. For the most part, a process needs to be mature before the manufacturer will even think about efficiency and becoming green. There are a number of certifications, but they are tricky. They usually focus on a specific area, say reduction of greenhouse gas emissions or energy usage. But that does not necessarily mean the product or process is truly green.

Conventional wisdom might suggest that going green will increase manufacturing costs, but the reality is that there is a cost benefit to going green. For example, greening your manufacturing processes can lead to an increase in energy efficiency, which means lower costs for energy per unit of production. Green manufacturing also implies more efficient transportation and distribution of raw materials, components and finished products, which means lower transport costs.

Manufacturers are evolving in the right direction. ISO 14000, for example, set environmental management standards. It is limited in scope, but it includes a commitment to continual improvements.

How important is green manufacturing for the industry and economy?
Extremely important. Green manufacturing also can be called efficient manufacturing. If U.S. manufacturers do not improve efficiencies year after year, we will lose our competitive edge. For me, it is not the branding of green that is important. It is the efficiency part that is important. It used to be that we focused on end-of-pipe solutions— treating the wastewater or emissions by installing something. In the last 10 to 15 years, the focus has shifted to the whole process, optimizing to avoid or minimize problems along the way, from start to finish.

Where do you see green manufacturing heading in the next five to 10 years?
Green manufacturing will only become more important over time. Right now the buzzwords are greenhouse gas emissions and energy supply. But there are other areas that are important, such as supply security, water, raw materials, and more. It is important to find the right balance. Any manufacturer can improve processes only to a given point. Then they will have to start looking at integrating with neighbors, suppliers, other industries; perhaps exporting waste heat. In the future, after the low-hanging fruit has been picked, manufacturers will need more creativity to help address these issues.

What career opportunities are there for someone to get into green manufacturing?
Jobs like environmental managers, process engineers, lean manufacturing managers. These are the individuals who look at the whole manufacturing process and can help make it more efficient. That may not sound green, but it is. From my perspective, it is important for someone to work in an industry that he or she is passionate about. It is the intimate knowledge of the specific industry and its processes that enables someone to make changes. There is no specific training for green manufacturing. An engineering degree is perfect. So are having broad knowledge and a critical mind to question information and assumptions. Always ask why: why this set point, why this equipment?

due in part to the sensitivity of union membership to the overall economic conditions of the country, to the trend towards white-collar employment—which is much less unionized than production-related occupations—and to the improvements in benefit packages offered in many industries. The movement of some manufacturing jobs overseas may also have an impact on the decline of union membership. There was a rise in overall union membership that took place in the 1960s and 1970s, but that was largely the result of the organization of employees in the public sector, not in private industries like manufacturing.

Union membership varies widely by industry sector. In 2006, computer and electronics manufacturing and the textile and apparel manufacturing, for example, had very low numbers of union memberships or employees covered by union contracts. About 5 percent of employees in the pharmaceutical and medicine industry and only 6 percent of employees in the printing industry were members of unions. Industries with the highest union membership (or employees covered by union contracts) were food manufacturing (19 percent), aerospace products and parts (21 percent), motor vehicles and parts (25 percent), and steel manufacturing (26 percent).

Current Trends

Medical technology develops with greater speed than most any other field. Being informed about up-to-date changes is essential if one is to advance in his or her career.

Nanotechnology

The nanoscale is one billionth of a meter, or one millionth of a millimeter. To get a sense of that: one sheet of paper is about 100,000 nanometers thick, a strand of blond hair is about 15,000 to 50,000 nanometers in diameter, and a strand of black hair is 50,000 to 180,000 nanometers in diameter. One advantage to nanoscale materials is that they often have different properties than the same material does at its regular, visible size. Manufacturers and scientists exploit these properties to create entirely new materials, and that is transforming the industry.

The National Nanotechnology Initiative, begun by the National Science Foundation, has identified four generations of nanotechnology.

The first began around 2000 and saw the rise of passive nanostructures like coatings, nanowires, and nanoparticles. The second generation, beginning around 2005, saw the rise of active nanostructures like transistors and targeted drugs and chemicals. The third generation is expected to begin about 2010, and will include developments in three-dimensional nanosystems and nanosystems that use synthesis and assembly techniques, such as bio-assembly, nanoscale robotics, and nanoscale networking. By 2015, the industry is projected to begin the fourth generation, with heterogeneous molecular nanosystems, where each molecule has a specific structure and role. This is the generation that will usher in fundamentally new functions from materials and structures. At that point, over 2 million people will be employed in the field. Engineers and scientists are needed to maintain innovation, and to help the United States claim a dominant and leadership position in the industry.

Nanotechnology both enables the use of new processes and materials in traditional manufacturing sectors, and opens the door for new, non-traditional products and processes. In 2003, the 21st Century Nanotechnology Research and Development Act (Public Law 108-153) was enacted. It calls for understanding nanoscale operations, developing a geographically dispersed network of facilities focused on nanotechnology, accelerating private industry R&D, encouraging research, providing effective education and training, and ensuring that ethical, legal, and environmental concerns are addressed.

Nanotechnology is becoming an efficient method for some types of manufacturing. Examples of nanotechnology applications in manufacturing include:

- advanced semiconductors
- nanobiotechnology and pharmaceutical applications like drug delivery and diagnostics
- sensors, filters, and other safety and security applications
- nanopowder-laden dispersions and suspensions in items like beauty products, paints, and additives
- coatings with nanopowder additives that make them resistant to abrasion and impermeable to oxygen and moisture, making them suitable for food and beverage packaging
- carbon nanotubes that are stronger than spider silk or Kevlar and, therefore, impact proof

- self-cleaning glass
- fabrics made from electrospinned plastic or ceramic fibers
- ultraviolet-resistant and water-repellant nanofilms for uses like computer screens or cameras
- carbon nanotubes for tennis racquets, flat panel televisions, and batteries
- computer transistors

Green Manufacturing

Green in the manufacturing industry is a journey, not an end state. Becoming a green manufacturer is more than recycling or instituting pollution control measures. It covers the gamut of environmentally friendly technologies, and includes limiting emissions of greenhouse gases, supporting the development of energy-efficient technologies, and minimizing the impact of manufacturing on the environment at all stages of the process.

Economic challenges have been one reason that manufacturing establishments have been more willing to consider environmental responsibility. As prices of raw materials and energy have increased, many seek new ways to reuse materials as a cost-saving measure. As end-users get more environmentally conscious and demand green products, manufacturers are responding to the shift in the market.

While the goal is admirable, it is still a challenge for many manufacturers. From the design to the transportation of the final product, there may be a large number of companies involved in the supply chain. For a product to truly be green, each part of the process and each manufacturer and supplier needs to be green. There are tradeoffs, too. Just-in-time inventory practices, for example, may mean that a shipment does not take up an entire truckload, but that means that more energy is used for shipping. Waiting for a truckload full of materials, however, may mean storing more inventory on site and slowing the production process or increasing costs.

General Conferences and Meetings

There are a number of conferences and meetings in each of the manufacturing sectors. Below are some industry-wide events and, following these, a sample of some of the sector-specific events. In addition to the sampling listed here, many industry trade associations host meetings, conferences, and other events.

Association of Manufacturing Excellence Conference Annual. Focus is on lean manufacturing processes and best practices. Sponsored by the Association for Manufacturing Excellence. (http://www.ame.org)

Nanobusiness Alliance Conference Annual. For professionals in manufacturing businesses impacted by nanotechnology, such as scientists and engineers. Focus is on industry trends and emerging technologies in various industry sectors. Sponsored by the Nanobusiness Alliance. (http://www.nanobusiness.org)

Society of Manufacturing Engineers Conference Annual. For manufacturers in all industries to discuss state of the industry, and emerging trends and technologies. Sponsored by the Society of Manufacturing Engineers. (http://www.sme.org)

Industry Specific Conferences and Meetings

Utilize the following conferences and meetings as opportunities to meet other professionals, forge friendships and lasting connections, and study up on cutting-edge manufacturing trends.

Food Manufacturing (NAICS 311)

Food Automation and Manufacturing Conference and Expo Annual. For those in the food and beverage processing and supplies business. Discussion of trends and technologies of manufacturing and food safety. Sponsored by *Food Engineering Magazine*. (http://www.foodengineeringmag.com)

International Baking Industry Exposition Annual. For bakers and manufacturers of baked goods. Focus is on sharing new technologies, equipment, and business solutions. Sponsored by the American Bankers Association and the Baking Industries Suppliers Association. (http://www.bakingexpo.org)

Institute of Food Technologists Annual Meeting and Food Expo Annual. For food scientists, food technologists, and other food industry professionals wanting to keep current on trends in the industry, including new products and technologies. Sponsored by the Institute of Food Technologists. (http://www.ift.org)

Beverage and Tobacco Product Manufacturing (NAICS 312)

InterBev Biennial. For beverage manufacturers and other industry professionals. Discussion of industry trends, operations, and sustainability. Sponsored by the American Beverage Association. (http://www.interbev.com)

Paper Manufacturing (NAICS 322)

PaperCon Annual. For engineers, management, and other professionals in the papermaking, coating, and graphic arts industries. Discussion of industry trends and technical topics. Sponsored by TAPPI. (http://www.papercon.org)

Chemical Manufacturing (NAICS 325)

American Chemical Society National Meeting and Exposition Biannual. For chemists, chemical engineers, students, and academics. Discussion of research and technical industry topics. Sponsored by the American Chemical Society. (http://www.acs.org)

Green Chemistry and Engineering Conference Annual. For scientists, engineers, and corporate leaders focused on sustainability and the chemical industry's transition to green products and processes. Sponsored by the American Chemical Society. (http://www.gcande.org)

Bio International Convention Annual. For people in the biotechnology industry. Discussion of industry trends, research, and policy. Sponsored by the biotechnology Industry Organization. (http://convention.bio.org)

International Good Manufacturing Practices Conference Annual. For production mangers, compliance and quality control personnel, and laboratory control personnel in the pharmaceutical industry. Discussion of drug and biological manufacturing issues, including FDA activities. (http://www.internationalgmp.com)

Plastics and Rubber Products Manufacturing (NAICS 326)

NPE Triennial. For manufacturers, materials and equipment providers, and other industry professionals. Discussion of technology, industry issues, and sector-specific issues. Sponsored by the Society of the Plastics Industry, Inc. (http://www.npe.org)

Nonmetallic Mineral Product Manufacturing (NAICS 327)

MINExpo   Quadrennial. Next meeting is scheduled for 2012. Discussion of materials, mining processes, and new technologies. Sponsored by the National Mining Association. (http://www.minexpo.com)

Machinery Manufacturing (NAICS 333)

PMMI Safety & Technology   Annual. For engineers, safety professionals, and management. Discussion of safety and technology, standards, and industry trends. Sponsored by the Packaging Materials Manufactures Institute. (http://www.pmmi.org)

Computer and Electronic Product Manufacturing (NAICS 334)

Custom Integrated Circuit Conference   Annual. For manufacturers of analog and digital circuits. Discussion of key industry issues and design. Sponsored by IEEE Solid-State Circuits Society. (http://www.ieee-cicc.org)

Transportation Equipment Manufacturing (NAICS 336)

Aerospace Manufacturing and Automated Fastening Conference and Exhibition   Annual. For manufacturers in aerospace and those interested in automated manufacturing and fastening. Discussion of technology and advancement of tools, materials, and processes. Sponsored by the SAE. (http://www.sae.org)

Major Manufacturing Companies

To give you a sense of the major players in manufacturing, below is a list of four to five companies in each industry sector, broken out by NAICS code. These companies are either U.S. owned or are U.S.

operating companies of foreign-owned or multinational firms. They are all within the top 20 in their industry sector and are listed here alphabetically.

Food Manufacturing (NAICS 311)

- Archer Daniels Midland   (http://www.admworld.com)
- General Mills   (http://www.generalmills.com)
- Inter-American Products
  (http://www.interamericanproducts.com)
- Kraft Foods   (http://www.kraftfoods.com)
- Tyson Foods   (http://www.tyson.com)

Beverage and Tobacco Product Manufacturing (NAICS 312)

- Anheuser Busch   (http://www.anheuser-busch.com)
- Coca-Cola Co.   (http://www.coca-cola.com)
- Lorillard Tobacco Co.   (http://www.lorillard.com)
- PepsiCo   (http://www.pepsico.com)
- Reynolds American   (http://www.reynoldsamerican.com)

Textile Mills (NAICS 313) and Textile Product Mills (NAICS 314)

- Albany International   (http://www.albint.com)
- Carters Inc.   (http://www.carters.com)
- Hanesbrands Inc.   (http://www.hanesbrands.com)
- Interface Inc.   (http://www.interfaceglobal.com)
- Mohawk Industries   (http://www.mohawkind.com)

Apparel Manufacturing (NAICS 315)

- Jones Apparel Group Inc.   (http://www.jonesapparel.com)
- Levi Strauss & Co.   (http://www.levistrauss.com)
- Liz Claiborne Inc.   (http://www.lizclaiborne.com)
- Polo Ralph Lauren Corp.   (http://www.ralphlauren.com)
- Quiksilver Inc.   (http://www.quiksilverinc.com)

Leather and Allied Product Manufacturing (NAICS 316)

- Coach Inc. (http://www.coach.com)
- Everett Smith Group Ltd. (http://www.esmithgroup.com)
- Timberland Co. (http://www.timberland.com)
- Wolverine World Wide Inc. (http://www.wolverineworldwide.com)

Wood Product Manufacturing (NAICS 321)

- Jeld-Wen Inc. (http://www.jeld-wen.com)
- Louisiana-Pacific Corp. (http://www.lpcorp.com)
- Masco Corp. (http://www.masco.com)
- Universal Forest Products Inc. (http://www.ufpi.com)

Paper Manufacturing (NAICS 322)

- International Paper Co. (http://www.ipaper.com)
- Kimberly-Clark Corp. (http://www.kimberly-clark.com)
- Meadwestvaco Corp. (http://www.meadwestvaco.com)
- Smurfit-Stone Container (http://www.smurfit.com)

Printing and Related Support Activities (NAICS 323)

- Gannett Co. Inc. (http://www.gannett.com)
- Idearc (http://www.idearc.com)
- Reed Elsevier (http://www.reed-elsevier.com)
- RR Donnelly & Sons (http://www.rrdonnelly.com)

Petroleum and Coal Products Manufacturing (NAICS 324)

- Chevron Corp. (http://www.chevron.com)
- Citgo Petroleum Corp. (http://www.citgo.com)
- ConocoPhillips (http://www.conocophillips.com)
- Koch Industries Inc. (http://www.kochind.com)
- Valero Energy Corp. (http://www.valero.com)

Chemical Manufacturing (NAICS 325)

- Abbott Laboratories (http://www.abbott.com)
- BASF (http://www.basf.com)
- Dow Chemical (http://www.dow.com)
- E. I. du Pont de Nemours & Co. (http://www.dupont.com)
- Pfizer Inc. (http://www.pfizer.com)

Plastics and Rubber Products Manufacturing (NAICS 326)

- Berry Plastics Corp (http://www.berryplastics.com)
- Goodyear Tire and Rubber Co. (http://www.goodyear .com)
- Graham Packaging Holdings (http://www .grahampackaging.com)
- Illinois Tool Works (http://www.itw.com)

Nonmetallic Mineral Product Manufacturing (NAICS 327)

- Oldcastle Inc. (http://www.oldcastle.com)
- Owens-Illinois Inc. (http://www.o-i.com)
- Saint-Gobain Corp. (http://www.saint-gobain-corporation .com)
- USG Corp. (http://www.usg.com)

Primary Metal Manufacturing (NAICS 331)

- Alcoa Inc. (http://www.alcoa.com)
- Arcelormittal USA (http://www.arcelormittal.com)
- Nucor Corp. (http://www.Nucor.com)
- United States Steel Corp. (http://www.ussteel.com)

Fabricated Metal Manufacturing (NAICS 332)

- American Axle & Manufacturing Holdings (http://www.aam.com)
- Ball Corp. (http://www.ball.com)

- Fortune Brands Inc. (http://www.fortunebrands.com)
- SPX Corp. (http://www.spx.com)
- Stanley Works (http://www.stanleyworks.com)

Machinery Manufacturing (NAICS 333)

- Caterpillar Inc. (http://www.cat.com)
- Cummins Inc. (http://www.cummins.com)
- Parker Hannifin Corp. (http://www.parker.com)
- United Technologies (http://www.utc.com)

Computer and Electronic Product Manufacturing (NAICS 334)

- Apple Inc. (http://www.apple.com)
- Cisco Systems Inc. (http://www.cisco.com)
- Emerson Electric (http://www.emerson.com)
- Northrop Grumman (http://www.northropgrumman .com)

Electrical Equipment, Appliance, and Component Manufacturing (NAICS 335)

- Eaton Corp. (http://www.eaton.com)
- L-3 Communications Corp. (http://www.l-3.com)
- Motorola (http://www.motorola.com)
- Texas Instruments (http://www.ti.com)
- Whirlpool Corp. (http://www.whirlpool.com)

Transportation Equipment Manufacturing (NAICS 336)

- Boeing Co. (http://www.boeing.com)
- General Dynamics (http://www.generaldynamics.com)
- General Motors (http://www.gm.com)
- Honeywell International (http://www.honeywell.com)
- Paccar Inc. (http://www.paccar.com)

Furniture and Related Product Manufacturing (NAICS 337)

- Hillenbrand Industries   (http://www.hillenbrand.com)
- HNI Corp.   (http://www.hnicorp.com)
- Johnson Controls   (http://www.johnsoncontrols.com)
- Leggett & Platt   (http://www.leggett.com)
- Steelcase Inc.   (http://www.steelcase.com)

Miscellaneous Manufacturing (NAICS 339)

- Armstrong World Industries Inc.   (http://www.armstrong.com)
- Blyth Inc.   (http://www.blyth.com)
- Edwards Lifesciences Corp.   (http://www.edwards.com)
- Josten's Inc.   (http://www.jostens.com)
- Mattel Inc.   (http://www.mattel.com)

General Organizations and Associations

There are a number of organizations and trade associations in each of the manufacturing sectors. Below are some industry-wide organizations and following those is a sample of some of the sector-specific groups.

Association of Manufacturing Excellence   Association dedicated to helping manufacturers with continuous improvement, through techniques such as lean tools, kaizen, and lean accounting. (http://www.ame.org)

Association for Operations Management   Organization focused on operations management, inventory, supply chain, and logistics. (http://www.apics.org)

Manufacturers Alliance   Industry organization that focuses on economic research, problem solving, and networking for senior executives in manufacturing. (http://www.mapi.net)

National Association of Manufacturers   Trade association that shares information with the public about manufacturing, focuses on policies and regulatory matters, and advocates for educational opportunities. (http://www.nam.org)

Sector-Specific Organizations and Associations

From providing tools to advance your career to advocacy and information related to safety, associations are ready resources for helping you establish and further your career interests across the manufacturing spectrum. They can be excellent for networking and for deepening your knowledge base of any sector that interests you.

Food Manufacturing (NAICS 311)

Institute of Food Technologists   Scientific organization for individuals in food science, food technology, and related industries. Advocates for policy, and provides education and research. (http://www.ift.org)

Food Processing Suppliers Association   Organization that represents suppliers of equipment, packaging, ingredients, and services to food, beverage, and pharmaceutical industries. Advocates for safety, and provides education and research. (http://www .fpmsa.org)

Keeping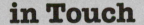
in Touch

Industry events are great opportunities to meet people in your industry and expand your network. Some tips:

- Have a plan of who you want to meet, which events you will attend, and how much time you will spend in the exhibit hall.

- If there is someone you are particularly interested in talking to and you know will be there, make an appointment in advance to meet for coffee or lunch.

- Bring your business cards, and hand them out.

- Talk to whomever you sit next to. It is one of the best ways of getting to know someone, without a lot of pressure.

- Follow-up with an e-mail or handwritten note, and maybe plan for future meetings or discussion.

American Bakers Association   Trade association for grain-based food industry. Promotes policy and represents interests of the wholesale baking industry before Congress, state legislatures, and international regulatory authorities. (http://www.americanbakers .org)

Baking Industry Suppliers Association   International trade association representing bakery and food equipment manufacturers, companies that provide ingredients, packaging materials and vehicles, and service providers including publishers, consultants, installers and financial services. Promotes technological advancement, education, safety, sanitation, marketing and good manufacturing practices. (http://www.bema.org)

Snack Food Association   Trade association for snack food manufacturers and suppliers. Provides education and research, advocates for the industry, and sponsors of snack trade show. (http://www.sfa.org)

Beverage and Tobacco Product Manufacturing (NAICS 312)

American Beverage Association   Organization for non-alcoholic beverage producers, distributors, and supporting industries. Advocates for the industry and sponsors the InterBev conference. (http://www.ameribev.org)

Textile Mills (NAICS 313), Textile Product Mills (NAICS 314), Apparel Manufacturing (NAICS 315)

Industrial Fabrics Association International   Trade association representing manufacturers and suppliers in specialty and technical textiles. Provides industry information and advocates for the industry. (http://www.iafi.com)

National Textile Association   Organization for manufacturers who knit and weave fabric, fiber suppliers, or other industry professionals. Provides industry and trade information and supports research and education. (http://www.nationaltextile.org)

Wood Product Manufacturing (NAICS 321)

American Forest and Paper Association   Trade association of the forest products industry, for mills, suppliers, and manufacturers of paper, pulp, paperboard, and wood products. Advocates for the industry and provides research and education. (http://www .afandpa.org)

Wood Flooring Manufacturers Association   Advocates for the industry, provides research and industry information, and establishes and enforces grade rules and quality standards. (http:// www.nofma.org)

Paper Manufacturing (NAICS 322)

Technical Association of Paper and Pulp Industry   Professional organization for the pulp, paper, and packaging industries. Provides information and education. Sponsors PaperCon annual conference. (http://www.tappi.org)

Printing and Related Support Activities (NAICS 323)

National Association of Printing Ink Manufacturers   Trade association for the ink industry. Provides research and technical information and advocates for the industry. (http://www.napim.org)

Printing Industries of America   Organization for printers, suppliers, and manufacturers. Advocates for the industry and provides education, research, and technical information. (http:// www.gain.org)

Petroleum and Coal Products Manufacturing (NAICS 324)

American Coal Council   Trade organization for coal suppliers, coal transportation companies, and coal service support firms. Advocates for the industry, and provides education and industry information. (http://www.clean-coal.info)

American Petroleum Institute   Trade association representing the oil and natural gas industry—producers, suppliers, operators, and suppliers. Provides industry information, education, policy advocacy. (http://www.api.org)

Chemical Manufacturing (NAICS 325)

American Chemistry Council   Organization of companies that work with chemicals. Focus is on protecting the environment, and protecting the health of workers and public. Divisions for plastics, chlorine chemistry, and chemical technology. (http://www.americanchemistry.com)

The Fertilizer Institute   Organization that promotes and protects fertilizer, from manufacturing to where it is used and everywhere in between. For manufacturers, retailers, wholesalers, and state fertilizer associations. Works to bring policy issues to legislators and the public. (http://www.tfi.org)

National Paint and Coating Association   In 2009 the organization merged with the Federation of Societies for Coatings Technology (www.coatingstech.org). Advocates for the industry and strengthens commitment to health, safety, and protection of the environment; and provides education and professional development. (http://www.paint.org)

Pharmaceutical Research and Manufa cturers of America (PhRMA)   Organization for pharmaceutical research and biotechnology companies. Advocates for the industry. (http://www.phrma.org)

Plastics and Rubber Products Manufacturing (NAICS 326)

Rubber Manufacturers Association   Trade association for manufacturers and suppliers of raw materials and equipment. Provides information on the market, government affairs, safety issues, and industry standards. (http://www.rma.org)

Society of the Plastics Industry, Inc.   Trade association representing the entire supply chain—manufacturers, materials and equipment suppliers, processors. Promotes business development, represents the industry, and works on sustainable growth in the industry. (http://www.plasticsindustry.org)

Vinyl Institute   Trade association advocating responsible manufacturing, life cycle management, and promotion of vinyl products. (http://www.vinylinfo.org)

Nonmetallic Mineral Product Manufacturing (NAICS 327)

National Mining Association   Trade organization representing the mining industry. Advocates for the industry. Gathers and makes available industry information and statistics. Sponsors MinExpo. (http://www.nma.org)

Primary Metal Manufacturing (NAICS 331) and Fabricated Metal Manufacturing (NAICS 332)

Aluminum Association   The association represents manufacturers and suppliers of aluminum and fabricated products. Develops and promotes industry standards, provides educational opportunities and research, and gathers industry statistics. (http://www.aluminum.org)

American Wire Producers Association   Represents manufacturers and distributors of wire, and materials and equipment suppliers in the Canada, Mexico, and the United States. Develops new market opportunities, conducts research and development, and provides technical data to its membership. (http://www.awpa.org)

Copper Development Association   Represents producers and fabricators of copper and copper alloys with facilities located in the United States. Provides industry, market, and technical information. (http://www.copper.org)

North American Die Casting Association   Represents industry members in Canada, Mexico, and the United States. Promotes industry awareness and growth of the market, and provides industry research and other resources. (http://www.diecasting.org)

Machinery Manufacturing (NAICS 333)

American Boiler Manufacturers Association   Association representing commercial, industry, and institutional boiler system manufacturers. Promotes understanding of the industry among government, manufacturers, and the public. (http://www.abma.com)

National Tooling and Machining Association   Organization for manufacturers of tools, dies, jigs, fixtures, special machines, and precision machined parts, in all industry sectors. Provides industry and market information, and education. (http://www.ntma.org)

Precision Machined Parts Association   Trade association for manufacturers of precision machined products. Provides industry and technical information, as well as education. (http://www.pmpa.org)

Computer and Electronic Product Manufacturing (NAICS 334)

The Technology Association of America Association representing interests of technology and electronics industries. Provides advocacy, research, and education. Created in 2009 from merger of American Electronics Association and the Information Technology Society of America. (http://www.itaa.org or http://www.aeanet.org)

Software and Information Industry Association Association for promoting industry interests, protecting intellectual property, information dissemination. For businesses who manufacture software, as well as distributors and publishers. (http://www.siia.net)

IPC Organization for manufacturers of printed circuit boards and electronics. Provides training, industry research, policy advocacy, and standard setting; while protecting the environment. (http://www.ipc.org)

Semiconductor Equipment and Materials International Organization for manufactures of microelectronics, displays, and photovoltaics. Provides education, standards development, policy, and industry information. Advocates for the industry. (http://www.semi.org)

Transportation Equipment Manufacturing (NAICS 336)

SAE Organization for engineers and scientists in the mobility technology sector—automotive and aerospace engineering. Provides standards and technical information, industry information and public awareness, and education. (http://www.sae.org)

Furniture and Related Product Manufacturing (NAICS 337)

Business and International Furniture Manufacturer's Association Organization for office and institutional furniture manufacturers. Provides standards and technical information, industry information, and education. Advocates for the industry. (http://www.bifma.com)

International Sleep Products Association Organization for mattress manufacturers and bedding component and machinery suppliers. Provides industry information and education, and advocates for the industry. (http://www.sleepproducts.org)

Miscellaneous Manufacturing (NAICS 339)

American Amusement Manufacturers Association   Trade organization for manufacturers, distributors, and parts suppliers in the coin-operated amusement industry. Provides industry information and education, and advocates for the industry. (http://www.coin-op.org)

Medical Device Manufacturers   Trade association for manufacturers of medical devices, diagnostic products, and healthcare information systems, and for other industry professionals. Provides industry information and education, and advocates for the industry. (http://www.medicaldevices.org)

Toy Industry Association   Trade association for producers and importers of toys. Provides education and safety information and industry research and trend information, and advocates for the industry. (http://www.toyassociation.org)

Standards Organizations

ISO   The International Organization for Standardization is a developer of international standards. An organization of organizations, its members are the national standards organizations of 161 countries. Compliance is voluntary—the organization has no legal authority. Develops and monitors international standards such as ISO 9001 (quality management) and ISO 14001 (environmental management systems), as well as industry-specific standards. (http://www.iso.org)

American National Standards Institute   United States standard organization and member of ISO. Oversees creation and use of norms and guidelines in businesses in every sector. (http://www.ansi.org)

Many industry organizations are responsible for voluntary, industry-specific standards. Some examples include: the American Society of Mechanical Engineers, the ASTM (formerly the American Society for Testing and Materials), the Data Interchange Standards Association, the Electronics Industries Association, the IEEE

(Institute of Electrical and Electronics Engineers), and the National Fire Protection Association.

U.S. Government Agencies

Many government agencies have oversight or regulatory responsibilities in the manufacturing industry and business operations. Below is a list of some of the major government organizations that manufacturing establishments typically interact with.

Consumer Products Safety Commission   An independent federal regulatory agency that protects the public from unreasonable risks of serious injury or death from the products under its jurisdiction like toys, household appliances (except those that emit radiation), and packaging. Develops, issues, and enforces standards, recalls products, and researches potential hazards. (http://www.cpsc.gov)

Environmental Protection Agency   Agency whose mission is to protect human health and the environment. Among other things, the agency develops and enforces regulations and studies environmental issues. Most businesses are affected by a number of environmental statutes and regulations. Relevant manufacturing industry sectors include: chemicals, electronics and computers, garments and textiles, leather products, metals, and pharmaceuticals. (http://www.epa.gov)

Export.gov   Government site to help U.S. businesses plan international sales strategies, get trade leads, and find relevant market research to aid in exporting. Run by several federal agencies. (http://www.export.gov)

Federal Maritime Commission   An independent regulatory agency that controls services, practices, and agreements of ocean-borne transportation. This agency is responsible for monitoring ports and common carriers that operate in the United States, and monitoring foreign regulations that may impact U.S. shipping conditions. (http://www.fmc.org)

Federal Trade Commission Agency that protects consumers from unfair, deceptive, or fraudulent practices by enforcing consumer protection laws and trade regulations. Regulates advertising for claims made by food, drugs, and dietary supplements, tobacco and alcohol, and computer and high-tech products and services. (http://www.ftc.gov)

Food Safety and Inspection Services Part of the U.S. Department of Agriculture. Responsible for ensuring the nation's commercial supply of meat, poultry, and egg products is safe, wholesome, and correctly labeled and packaged. (http://www.fsis.usda.gov)

International Trade Administration   Agency of the U.S. Department of Commerce. Designed to promote trade and compliance with trade laws. The Manufacturing and Services unit analyzes trade policy, builds capacity, and works to advance U.S. manufacturers. Through the Manufacturing Initiative (www.manufacturing.gov), the administration addresses challenges specific to U.S. manufacturers. Contains links to relevant industry associations. (http://www.ita.doc.gov)

National Highway Transportation Safety Agency   Agency of the Department of Transportation. Works to prevent injuries and reduce the economic costs due to road traffic crashes, through education, research, safety standards, and enforcement. Develops and enforces manufacturing standards for motor vehicles and motorcycles. (http://www.nhtsa.gov)

National Institute of Standards and Technology Non-regulatory agency of the U.S. Department of Commerce. Promotes U.S. innovation and industrial competitiveness by advancing measurement science, standards, and technology. Conducts research, promotes excellence through the Baldrige National Quality Program, offers technical and business assistance to smaller manufacturers, and runs the Technology Innovation Program. (http://www.nist.gov)

National Nanotechnology Initiative   A government project involving the individual and cooperative nanotechnology-related activities of 25 federal agencies. The goal of the project is to advance research, develop educational resources, and provide for technology transfer. (http://www.nano.gov)

Occupational Safety and Health Administration   Agency of the U.S. Department of Labor. Works to ensure safe and healthful work conditions by establishing and enforcing standards, and providing research, education, and training. Specific safety and health topics for manufacturing sectors like apparel, meatpacking, nanotechnology, steel, and wood products. (http://www.osha.gov)

Surface Transportation Board   Agency of the U.S. Department of Transportation. Regulates and enforces rates for railroads, certain trucking companies, certain pipelines, and non-contiguous ocean shipping companies. Formerly the Interstate Commerce Commission. (http://www.stb.dot.gov)

U.S. Chemical Safety Board   Independent agency that investigates chemical accidents and makes recommendations to plants, regulatory agencies, industry organizations, and labor groups. (http://www.chemsafety.gov)

U.S. Food and Drug Administration   An agency of the U.S. Department of Health and Human Services. Protects the public health by assuring the safety, efficacy, and security of human and veterinary drugs, biological products, medical devices, food, cosmetics, and radiation-emitting products. Establishes product and manufacturing standards in areas like biologics, drugs, medical devices, and radiation-emitting devices like microwave ovens, x-ray equipment, and laser products. Regulates labeling of cosmetics, drugs, and food products, as well as advertising for prescription drugs and medical devices. (http://www.fda.gov)

Chapter 3

On the Job

Most manufacturing facilities, no matter the size or industry sector, operate in roughly the same way in terms of workflow. First a product is designed. Then it is produced and checked for quality. Then it is either shipped to the customer or put into inventory to await distribution. While those things are happening, health, safety, and environment professionals are making sure the facility and employees are following the proper safety processes. The maintenance teams are ensuring the facilities and equipment are in working order. And the administrative professionals are making sure the business stays viable by marketing and selling the products, maintaining the finances, hiring employees, and managing the entire organization.

There is no standard organizational chart for manufacturing establishments. Each company bases its reporting structure and hierarchy on the needs of manufacturing activities they are engaged in, the materials being manufactured, the size of the company, and the management style of the executives.

In this chapter, you will find a list of common positions across the manufacturing industry, organized by department and presented in the order outlined above.

Design and Development

Every product starts with an idea in someone's head. Then it is designed, a prototype is made from the design drawings and specifications, and the product is tested and refined before it is mass-produced. Most large manufacturing companies have their own design and development departments.

Designer, Commercial and Industrial

Designers are responsible for all aspects of the products they design, from appearance and function to safety and quality. The design process includes developing a new design or altering an existing one, researching customer needs and how the product will be used, illustrating the product with sketches or diagrams, modeling or prototyping the product, and testing it and making adjustments. Designers are expected to use computer-aided design (CAD) software. Some designers specialize in a particular product or category such as appliances, medical equipment, toys, or housewares.

Designers work with engineers, materials scientists, production teams, the sales and marketing staff, and accountants. Designers typically spend one to three years in a job before advancing to a supervisory position or leaving a manufacturing establishment to start their own design firm. Advancement usually includes managing design department staff members.

Entry-level designers typically have a bachelor's degree in a field like industrial design, architecture, or engineering. Some have a master's degree in industrial design or an MBA, but that is not necessary for getting into the field.

Food Scientist

Food scientists create and improve food products. They use their knowledge of science to develop better ways of preserving, processing, packaging, storing, and delivering foods. That may include research to discover new food sources or substitutes for harmful additives, analyzing food content to determine levels of nutrients, or improving processes. Food scientists work with other scientists, generally in a laboratory or test kitchen, but sometimes in an office.

Depending on the plant and the particular job responsibilities, food scientists may be considered part of the production team or part of the development team. Food scientists typically advance to manager or supervisor or move from production to positions in research and development. Entry-level employees typically have a bachelor's degree in science, chemistry, or a related field. Some may have a master's degree, but that is not necessary to get into the field.

Laboratory Assistant

In biotechnology, pharmaceutical, and other chemical and medical related companies, these are the individuals who assist with research and experiments. They collect and interpret data, write reports, and maintain laboratory equipment. They work with research scientists. Entry-level lab technicians have an associate's degree in science, chemistry, or a related field, as well as experience in a laboratory setting. Some companies require a bachelor's degree in chemistry or science.

Model Maker

These are the individuals who create the molds used to make products like candles, jewelry, toys, and some types of food. In woodworking, model makers cut, shape, and plane surfaces to create models and molds. They work with detailed instructions and specifications and are expected to use computer-aided design (CAD) software. Entry-level model makers usually have a high school diploma or GED, then receive substantial on the job training. Some study via apprenticeships.

Tool and Die Maker

Considered the most highly skilled workers in a manufacturing plant, tool and die makers create the parts for machines used in the production process, such as tools, dies, guiding or holding devices, or jigs. Machinists typically make a single part. But tool and die makers make many parts and have a thorough knowledge of machining properties like hardness and heat tolerance. They often

Best Practice

Getting Promoted

Here are some things to think about if you want to take the next step up the corporate ladder:

- Challenge yourself with difficult or complex projects.
- Come up with and implement innovative and creative ideas.
- Take advantage of training and educational opportunities
- Find a mentor to show you the ropes.
- Take responsibility for your failures and learn from them.
- Take credit for your successes, without bragging, and learn from them.

use computer-aided design (CAD) software and computer numeri-cally controlled (CNC) machines.

Tool and die makers usually work in tool rooms that are clean and generally quieter than the production floor, but often they must wear safety equipment. They advance to CNC programmers or, for those with degrees, engineering or tool design. Entry-level tool and die makers have a high school diploma or GED and four to five years of training via a community college, technical school, or on the job. Some study via an apprenticeship.

Software Architect

This is the person who designs the components and interface for software applications. They describe how the software will work, and may have responsibility for deployment and implementation, as well. Software architects must understand multiple programming languages, as well as operating systems and computing platforms. Entry-level software architects have a bachelor's degree and pro-gramming experience or industry certification, or have begun their career as programmers.

Production and Quality Assurance

Once the product is designed and approved, someone has to make it. That is where the production teams come in. No matter how the product is made, this is the heart of most manufacturing plants. The quality assurance personnel ensure that the product is created to specifications and is safe and worth what the customer is going to pay for it.

Assembler

These are the individuals who put the final product together, using tools or their hands. Because they work directly with the product, they also look for and remove faulty components. That makes them a key piece of the quality process, in addition to their production responsibilities. Team assemblers work in small groups, especially in companies that use lean manufacturing systems. Each team mem-ber is trained in all the assembly tasks and they rotate through them. Assemblers may be called fabricators, or a title specific to what is being assembled, such as: electronic equipment assembler, fiberglass fabricator, or timing device assembler.

With their experience working directly with a company's product, assemblers have many advancement opportunities. They advance to machinist or CNC programmer, or to positions in product repair or maintenance, quality control, research and development, or product design. Advancement within production usually includes supervising or managing other assemblers. Entry-level assemblers typically have a high school diploma or GED. In some industries, such as aircraft manufacturing, assemblers must have an associate's degree or other advanced training.

Baker

Bakers are a type of food processor. They mix and bake ingredients to produce baked goods such as bread, cake, or cookies. They use their knowledge of food production techniques and equipment, storage and handling, raw materials, production processes, and quality control. Bakers advance to supervisors or to management. Entry-level bakers typically have a high school degree or GED.

Calibration Technician

These are the technicians who develop and test calibration and related processes, including lubrication, cleaning, and adjustment of measuring devices. In some companies, these technicians have responsibility for quality control, and in others they conduct research and develop new procedures. They are expected to understand the regulatory guidelines for the industry sector they work in.

Entry-level calibration technicians typically have a high school diploma or GED and several years of experience. Some companies require an associate's degree in engineering technology, industrial mechanics, or a related field, and experience working with instrumentation.

Computer Control Programmer

These programmers develop programs for the machine tools in a factory. They use the blueprints and specifications for a product to develop the proper sequence of events to fabricate the product, including where cuts should occur and at what speed. They may also be called numerical tool and process control programmers.

Computer control programmers typically work on computers near the shop floor and must wear proper safety equipment when they visit production areas. They work with assemblers, machinists, and machine operators. Computer control programmers advance to supervisory or administrative roles.

Entry-level computer control programmers typically worked as machine operators, machinists, or assemblers; or have a high school diploma or GED and training via a community college or technical school. Some study via an apprenticeship. In some industries, such as aerospace, computer control programmers must have a bachelor's degree in engineering.

Food Processor

As the name suggests, a person with this job processes raw food into the finished product. Batchmakers are food processors that operate mixing and blending equipment. Cooking machine operators operate equipment like pressure cookers, kettles, or deep-fry cookers. In the meat industry, these processors usually work in an assembly line and may be called slaughterers, meat packers, cutters, or trimmers. Their job is to convert animal carcasses into smaller pieces of meat and pack it for distribution.

The conditions in which food processors work varies depending on the industry, type of job, and size of the establishment. Safety is a primary concern for all food processing jobs. Food processors advance to team leaders, supervisors, or department managers. Entry-level food processors typically have a high school degree or GED and on the job training. Some study via an apprenticeship. In some companies, a bachelor's degree is helpful for advancement to a supervisory position.

Machinist

People who work as machinists produce metal parts, often one-of-a-kind items or in small batches. Machinists position a piece on the machine, set the controls, and monitor the equipment speed and performance as well as the final product, often to maintain the proper temperature while the metal cools. They use tools like lathes, shapers, and grinders. Many machine tools are computer numerically controlled (CNC), and follow a program to control the cutting. Machinists who use these machines can also be called computer control operators.

Machinists work near sophisticated and sometimes dangerous equipment and often must wear protective equipment like safety shields and earplugs. Machinists advance to computer control programmers, tool and die makers, mold makers, or into a supervisory role.

Entry-level machinists typically worked as assemblers, machine setters, or operators; they typically have a high school diploma or GED and on the job training or training via a community college or technical school. Some study via an apprenticeship that can last up to four years.

Metal Fabricator

These are individuals who create metal items with processes like cutting, hammering, welding, bending, and pressing. Metal fabricators read and create blueprints and product specifications. They may need to reprogram the computer programs running the equipment they operate. The work can be highly automated and repetitive, depending on the industry.

Metal fabricators work with complex equipment and often must wear protective equipment. Sometimes they work with computer control operators. They advance to supervisory roles. Entry-level metal fabricators typically have a high school diploma or GED and on the job training or training via a community college or technical school. Some study via an apprenticeship that can last up to five years.

Quality Control Inspector

These inspectors check products—from raw materials to finished goods—and ensure they measure up to the standards of the company, the industry, and all applicable government regulations. In the food industry, quality control inspectors may taste items, in other industries they may put a product on a form and look for defects, in others they select a random sample and test with gauges. They must also verify that the physical characteristics of the product are correct—color, weight, texture, and correctly fitting parts. Some inspectors work on computers in offices and others work on the production floor, with the product in hand.

Quality control inspectors work with production employees at all stages in the process. They advance to materials or equipment purchasers, into positions inspecting more complex products, or they become supervisors and manage quality control staff. Certification from an organization like the American Society for Quality may help advancement.

In some manufacturing sectors, entry-level quality control inspectors typically have a high school diploma or GED and in-house training, as well as experience in jobs such as assembler or machine operator. In other sectors, entry-level inspectors have an associate's degree and experience with CAD or specifically in a production environment or laboratory.

Production Manager

The production manager is responsible for coordinating the people and processes required for production, including making sure that quality and output goals are met. Some production managers are responsible for one area of a plant, but others oversee the entire facility. Production managers work closely with many other departments such as sales, logistics, and finance, and they usually work in the production area or an office. Production managers advance to a high level of management, such as plant manager or vice president of manufacturing.

Entry-level production managers have a bachelor's degree in business, management, or an engineering discipline, as well as experience in production or operations. Some manufacturers require that production managers have a master's degree.

Semiconductor Technician

Microchips are everywhere these days, and someone has to make them. Semiconductor technicians are the people who do this. They use automated equipment and work in cleanrooms—production areas kept free of all airborne matter, as even microscopic particles are able to damage the tiny circuitry. They work with toxic chemicals, as well. As a result, these technicians must wear special protective garments in the cleanroom. Semiconductor manufacturing occurs around the clock, so some technicians must work night shifts.

Semiconductor technicians advance to have greater responsibility or to become senior technicians, leading a team or working with engineers. Entry-level technicians may start out as machine opera-tors, starting and monitoring the production equipment. A certif-icate or associate's degree is required to become a semiconductor technician.

Solderer

Solderers join metal pieces together using molten metal. This is com-mon in joining electrical, electronic, or other small metal pieces. Sol-derers use drawings and specifications to determine the best way to join the pieces. The job can be hazardous, as the metals used in the soldering process are typically near 800 degrees Fahrenheit. Safety equipment and proper ventilation is required for these workers.

Solderers advance to supervisors or inspectors. Entry-level sol-derers typically have a high school diploma or GED, and training via a vocational school or community college. Solderers are expected to have good eyesight and manual dexterity, in addition to an under-standing of electricity and computers.

Engineering jobs

Engineers are involved in different functions in a manufacturing environment. They use their analytical skills, creativity, and orien-tation to detail to design and develop new products and machinery, test manufactured products, or work in production. Entry-level engi-neers have a bachelor's degree in an engineering discipline, but it is not unusual for someone in an engineering field to have a degree in science or mathematics instead. A person in this field can advance to become a technical specialist, a supervisor, or move into a mana-gerial or sales role. Continuing education is a key to advancement in engineering jobs, as information changes rapidly in some fields, such as biotechnology or information technology.

Biomedical Engineer

These individuals design and develop medical and health-related products such as artificial organs, prostheses, instruments, medi-cal information systems, and various medical devices. In addition to a degree in an engineering specialty like mechanical engineering, biomedical engineers also have specialized biomedical engineering training.

Chemical Engineer

These engineers work for large-scale chemical manufacturers, as well as for other manufacturing sectors that require chemicals such as energy, apparel, food, and paper manufacturing. Some chemical engineers specialize in one chemical process, others specialize in a particular field, like nanotechnology. Others focus on a specific product. Chemical engineers advance to jobs such as environment, health, and safety manager, or to other management positions. Depending on the industry sector they work in, chemical engineers may be called engineering scientists, process development engineers, or refinery process engineers.

Engineering Manager

Engineering managers usually work in an office, and plan and coordinate activities in engineering or research and development departments. In addition, they are responsible for management tasks like supervising employees, preparing budgets and contracts, and project management. An engineering manager may also be called principal engineer, project engineer, or project manager.

Industrial Engineer

Manufacturing a product involves many aspects to be managed, such as people, machines, materials, energy use, and safety, to name a few. Industrial engineers are the people who spend their days thinking about how to manage these things. They study design requirements and design systems to meet them. They work with management control systems to analyze production costs. They design systems to coordinate production activities with quality assurance.

Industrial engineers work closely with the business side of the company and often advance to management or executive positions. They are also called manufacturing engineers, manufacturing specialists, process engineers, or production engineers.

Materials Engineer

Products of all types use special materials like metals, ceramics, plastics, and composites. Materials engineers are the people who design and develop these new materials. Most specialize in a type of material, such as metal or ceramics.

Mechanical Engineer

In some ways, this is an engineering generalist. Mechanical engineers work with tools, machines, engines, and other mechanical devices like generators or robots. They also design tools that other engineers use in their work. Typical job tasks include reading blueprints and technical specifications, and researching and analyzing products and equipment. They may also be called equipment engineers or product engineers.

Product Development Engineer

These engineers design and develop existing products and processes—from start to finish, from idea to reality. In addition to basic design, a key function of a product development engineer is to ensure safety and quality. This job is common in the biotechnology sector.

On the Cutting
Edge

Nanotechnologist

These are the individuals who develop, design, and manipulate nanomaterials for products like computers, robots, food, clothing, and coatings. In food science, nanotechnologists do things like develop sensors to detect contaminants in food. In the textile industry, nanotechnologists help design original fibers and specialty garments using nanomaterials. Much of the work in nanotechnology is still in the research phase and there are not many applications yet.

Entry-level nanotechnologists need an associate's or bachelor's degree, depending on the industry. Chemical engineers who work in nanotechnology are required to have a bachelor's degree. It is estimated that in the next 15 years, 2 million workers will be needed to support nanotechnology industries worldwide.

Sales Engineer

Understanding scientifically or technically advanced products requires in-depth technical skills. Sales engineers act as sales representatives, or they team up with sales representatives to sell products. They may act as consultants to the production, engineering, or research departments to help design or modify the product to meet customer needs. Many sales engineers specialize based on their engineering discipline—a chemical engineer might sell chemical products, for example. Their duties are often similar to other sales reps.

Advancement for sales engineers is similar to that of a standard sales representative: a higher commission rate or larger territory, promotion to supervisor, or a move to marketing management.

Inventory and Distribution

Raw materials must be gathered before a product can be manufactured. Once it is made, the product is then stored until it leaves the facility for the next step in the process—another manufacturer, in the case of a component product, or to a wholesaler or retailer in the case of a finished product. Inventory and distribution personnel are involved in the acquisition, storage, and management of the raw materials used in the process, as well as in the disbursement of the final product.

Inventory Control Manager

Managing the inventory of products, parts, and raw materials is the job of the inventory control manager. This is the person responsible for tracking both incoming and finished goods. This job function is often automated, with computerized inventory control systems, automatic stackers and conveyor belts, and automated, driverless vehicles that retrieve goods. This job occasionally requires lifting and moving of heavy materials.

Inventory control managers work primarily with others in the inventory process, such as stock clerks and order fillers. Some have department management responsibilities. Additional education is often required for advancement. Entry-level inventory control managers typically have a high school diploma or GED, and some level of computer or business experience. Some manufacturers may require an associate's or bachelor's degree and some level of experience, such as stock clerk.

Logistics Specialist

Management of shipping is a job for the logistics staff in a manufacturing facility. They take care of the whole process, from booking the loads to tracking the delivery. They are responsible for costs and equipment, as well as planning for transportation, managing relationships with customers and shippers, and taking care of customs and warehousing. In some companies, the logistics specialist also performs inventory controls tasks.

Entry-level logistics specialists usually have two to five years of experience in areas like logistics, inventory management, freight forwarding, or purchasing. Many manufacturers require either a bachelor's degree in business, industrial engineering, or logistics, or a certification in supply chain management or logistics. Some companies require logistics specialists to be licensed customs brokers.

Packaging Manager

Every product, whether it is being shipped to a wholesaler or retailer, or to another manufacturer for further processing, must be packaged and labeled for shipping. The packaging manager is the person responsible for overseeing that part of the operation. This is the person who manages the daily operations and the packaging staff, including shipping clerks. This person ensures that the process is done safely and efficiently, and may also have responsibility for quality issues.

Entry-level packaging managers have a bachelor's degree in business or a related area, experience in batch processing or customer support, and an understanding of applicable standards and regulations.

Purchasing Agent

Purchasing agents are the individuals responsible for buying the raw materials and supplies that are critical to the efficient and profitable operation of a manufacturing facility. They research suppliers, searching for the best quality and price, they analyze financial information, and they purchase materials and merchandise. They usually focus on routine purchasing tasks or specialize in one particular commodity or material.

Purchasing agents advance to purchasing managers, with managerial and department wide responsibilities. They usually have a bachelor's degree in business, economics, or accounting. In some companies, purchasing agents are called procurement specialists.

Purchasing Manager

Like purchasing agents, purchasing managers are responsible for acquiring supplies like machinery, raw materials, and fabricated parts. The purchasing manager usually handles the more complex or critical purchasing tasks, as well as supervising purchasing agents. In addition, purchasing managers typically travel as part of the job, including visiting suppliers and distributors. Purchasing managers are often involved in product development, to help with determination of suitable materials and the associated costs.

A graduate degree is sometimes required for advancement to the management level. Certification in supply management, purchasing, or operations management can help a purchasing manager advance as well. Entry-level purchasing managers have bachelor's degrees in business, accounting, economics, or even engineering; they are also expected to take in-house training. They are sometimes called merchandise managers.

Shipping and Receiving Clerk

Like logistics specialists, shipping the finished product is the primary job of shipping and receiving clerks. They work in the warehouse, directly handling the goods, which means they may have to drive the forklift or load or unload shipments. They ship and receive goods, maintain records of inventory, and may even do some of the packaging in smaller establishments.

With extensive experience or additional training, shipping and receiving clerks can advance to shipping and receiving manager or to distribution manager. Entry-level clerks usually have a high school diploma or GED.

Shipping and Receiving Manager

This employee is responsible for the entire shipping department or distribution center. They supervise drivers, shipping and receiving clerks, and other employees. The job includes management of transportation and distribution strategies as well as the budget.

Entry-level shipping and receiving managers typically have bachelor's degree in business or a related field. They also have five to ten years of experience in warehouses or distribution, or an equivalent amount of experience as a shipping and receiving clerk. In some companies, export experience is necessary to advance to this management position.

Storage and Distribution Manager

This is the individual responsible for the raw materials and parts that have arrived at the facility and for the finished product once it is ready to be distributed. This manager is responsible for truck drivers, all the packaging and shipping operations, scheduling deliveries, ensuring compliance with safety and other regulations, and quality control.

Entry-level storage and distribution managers have a bachelor's degree in engineering, logistics, or finance, and at least five years of warehouse or other distribution experience, such as shipping and receiving clerk.

Supply Chain Manager

This job requires an understanding of all areas of the supply chain—sourcing, procurement, purchasing, warehousing, distribution, transport, budgeting, and sales. It is the supply chain manager's job to forecast demand and manage the inventory, manage supplier relationships, and supervise employees. Supply chain managers work closely with logistics and purchasing personnel, and in some companies may be responsible for those jobs as well.

Supply chain managers report to the management or executive level and can advance to that level, as well. Entry-level supply chain managers have a bachelor's degree and experience in logistics, warehousing, or distribution. Some companies require experience with global operations or logistics.

Traffic Manager

This distribution support position is responsible for managing shipping systems and vendors, outbound and inbound logistics issues, overseeing transportation procedures, and coordinating the shipping equipment and schedules. The traffic manager must be familiar with U.S. Department of Transportation regulations, and all other applicable standards and regulations. This job involves management of shipping or warehouse personnel.

Entry-level traffic managers often start out as shipping and receiving clerks, or have a bachelor's degree in business, supply chain management, or a related field. Experience in supply chain or transportation management is a plus. Some companies prefer employees with a master's degree.

Warehouse Manager

The warehouse manager is in charge of all warehouse employees and operations. They are responsible for the process of order fulfillment, ensuring vehicles are available and in compliance, and ensuring quality and safety. The job very often entails physical lifting or moving of materials.

Entry-level warehouse managers typically have a high school diploma or GED, as well as computer skills, distribution or warehouse experience, and often some supervisory experience. Some companies require a bachelor's degree for this position.

Health, Safety, and Environment

During the manufacturing process, someone must make sure that the facility, its systems, and the manufacturing processes are designed and conducted in a way that protects the health and safety of the employees. Health, safety, and environmental specialists are the individuals who do this.

Environment, Health, and Safety Manager

This is the individual who ensures that the company and its processes comply with applicable corporate, local, state, and federal regulations and standards. The environment, health, and safety managers also lead employee safety teams. Entry-level managers typically have a bachelor's degree in environmental science, occupational safety, or chemical engineering. Some start out as environmental protection specialists and move into this management role. Certification in health, safety, and environmental science is beneficial for advancement to this position.

Environmental Science and Protection Technician

These technicians are responsible for activities like collecting and testing air and water samples, helping the company provide proper protection for its employees, assuring regulatory compliance, and writing reports. This individual may work in an office, but may also have to go out into the field for testing and other activities. In some plants, this individual may be responsible for inspections or hazardous waste storage facilities.

Environmental science and protection technicians advance to management roles, including environment, health, and safety managers. Entry-level technicians have a bachelor's degree in environmental engineering, environmental science, or a related field, or they have an associate's degree in one of those fields combined with experience in areas like safety, environmental permits or inspections, or with ISO 14001. In some companies, these technicians are called environmental analysts, environmental health specialists, or health environmentalists.

Process Control Technician

This is the person who manages processes in the entire facility or within a specific area such as a laboratory, and ensures that the finished product adheres to all applicable standards, regulations, and quality requirements. Job responsibilities include data acquisition and analysis, managing software licenses and updates, review of industry and customer process standards, and training production or inspection personnel.

The process control technician often manages process improvement teams and process-related projects. In facilities that operate 24 hours a day, the process control technician may have to work the night shift. Entry-level technicians typically have an associate's degree in industrial technology or a related field. Some employers require a bachelor's degree instead.

Quality Auditor

The quality auditor is responsible for making sure that the finished product does what it is supposed to do. In the apparel industry, for example, a quality auditor may test the garments to ensure they hold up for washing. In the food industry, the quality auditor may taste test a product or ensure that it includes the right amount of a particular ingredient—he or she may confirm that there are enough nuts in the ice cream, for example.

Quality auditors advance to management or possibly to regulatory positions like regulatory manager. Entry-level quality auditors have at least a high school diploma or GED. Some employers require a bachelor's degree, and others look for certification in quality auditing.

Quality Assurance Manager

This is the person in a manufacturing establishment who is responsible for all the quality activities. In some companies, the quality assurance manager may also have responsibility for environmental and health and safety activities. This job requires a knowledge of industry and governmental regulations, as well as quality programs. Quality assurance managers may develop and maintain quality controls and documentation and even work directly with customers to ensure compliance. They also manage quality auditors and other staff. In some companies, regulatory management is the responsibility of the quality assurance manager.

Entry-level quality assurance managers have a bachelor's degree in quality or a technical subject applicable to the industry sector they work in. Most employers also require at least five years of experience in a management or quality assurance activity. Some employers require certification in quality auditing.

Regulatory Manager

Some manufacturing businesses like biotech, medical, or chemical companies need a regulatory manager to understand regulatory requirements and to work with appropriate government and regulatory agencies. This individual coordinates with the development, production, and quality teams to ensure compliance with regulatory requirements at all stages of product development and manufacturing. They typically spend time in an office, but depending on the company, they also may work in a laboratory environment or on the production floor.

Entry-level regulatory managers have a bachelor's degree in science, chemistry, biology, or a related field. Companies typically look for employees with experience working with regulatory agencies and with quality auditing. Some companies, especially in the

Problem
Solving

Industrial Safety

An equipment manufacturer uses grinding machines in their production process, potentially putting employees at risk of injuries like broken bones or crushed fingers. The company trains new employees in operating the machines safely and has a written safety manual that all employees were required to read.

Tim, the new machinist, read the safety manual first. Then his supervisor trained him briefly in operating the machine, and left him alone to get started. Tim noticed that the machine next to his had a guard in front of the grinder, and that the other employee had earplugs. The environment was loud and, even though he had read the safety manual, Tim didn't feel comfortable operating the machinery without the guard or other safety equipment. But he didn't know what to do or who to talk to.

It is the job of the health and safety personnel and plant management to ensure that all production equipment is operated safely and properly. But it is also the job of each employee to look out for his or her own safety. Speak up if you do not feel that you understand how to use the equipment safely or if you do not have the proper safety equipment. Talk to your manager or go directly to the safety coordinators or managers. It could be a simple thing—that somehow the guard was removed during a routine repair and the fact that it was missing was overlooked in the last safety review. It could also be that the company does not work hard enough to provide a safe workplace. If it is the latter, you will want to consider a new place of employment. If it is the former, your supervisor and the safety managers will thank you for bringing it to their attention. A safe workplace is the goal of all successful manufacturers.

pharmaceutical sector, want employees with experience working a in cleanroom environment.

Safety Coordinator

This is the individual who conducts routine safety inspections and makes recommendations for improvements. He or she investigates any safety-related incidents or accidents, documents safety information, and helps educate employees about safety issues. Safety coordinators are knowledgeable about applicable government regulations and enforce regulatory compliance. In pharmaceutical and food processing, they apply good manufacturing practices.

This person may be responsible for managing environment, health, and safety personnel. In some companies this job may be the same as, or a backup to, the environment, health, and safety manager. Entry-level safety coordinators typically have a bachelor's degree or equivalent safety experience and certification.

Installation, Maintenance, and Repair

All manufacturing facilities have equipment and machinery of some sort, typically on the production floor to make the finished product. In addition, some manufacturers create products that require installation or ongoing service or repair. Installation, maintenance, and repair personnel take care of the machinery and equipment. On the production side, they ensure smooth processes and timely delivery of finished goods. On the customer service side, they ensure that customers are satisfied with the product and its performance.

Electrical and Electronics Repairer, Commercial and Industrial

There are a tremendous number of electronic devices and machines in a modern manufacturing plant. Electrical and electronics repairers are the individuals who install and set up these devices, test them, and fix them when they break. The job requires a thorough knowledge of electrical circuits and transistors, the ability to read blueprints, diagrams, and specifications, the ability to do very physical labor, and good hand eye coordination to work with small components.

In companies that operate three shifts, electrical repairers may have to work night shifts. The job can be dangerous and has strict safety procedures. Entry-level electrical and electronics repairers typically have an associate's degree in electronics or a technical field, especially in industry sectors like medical equipment and devices. In addition to experience and education, electrical and electronics repairers must have good color vision to identify electrical wires by color.

Electrician

In a manufacturing environment, electricians do complex maintenance work such as repairing motors, generators, or electronic controls on machine tools or industrial robots. They also inspect equipment and ensure that it remains in working order. Like electrical and electronics repairers, they may also install and set up this machinery. Electricians work with engineers and engineering technicians, electrical and electronics repairers, and industrial machinery mechanics. In companies that operate 24 hours a day, electricians may have to work night shifts. The job can be dangerous and has strict safety procedures.

Electricians advance to supervisory positions or become inspectors. Entry-level electricians have a high school diploma or GED. Some study via an apprenticeship program. In most areas, electricians must pass a test about electricity and electrical codes to become licensed by the state or municipality. In addition to experience and education, electricians must have good color vision to identify electrical wires by color.

Industrial Machinery Mechanic

Like the name suggests, industrial machinery mechanics are responsible for maintaining and repairing the machinery in a manufacturing facility. To do this, they use technical manuals, observation, and an understanding of the equipment to diagnose and fix problems. Industrial machinery mechanics work closely with electricians or electronics repairers. In addition to performing repairs, industrial machinery mechanics order replacement parts and keep detailed records of the machines and their performance.

The work of maintaining industrial machines is dangerous and industrial machinery mechanics often are required to wear safety equipment like steel-toed shoes, hearing protectors, safety glasses, and hard hats. Overtime is common since machinery must be in service for production to take place. Some industrial machinery mechanics specialize in a particular area, such as hydraulics.

Industrial machinery mechanics advance to jobs taking care of more complicated equipment. They may also advance to master mechanic, millwright, or supervisory positions. Entry-level mechanics have a high school diploma or GED and typically some additional education to gain mechanical and technical experience. They are expected to have electrical, electronics, or computer programming skills experience. Additional training may be through an apprenticeship, an associate's degree, or the military. Some mechanics start out as assistants and learn on the job. In some companies, the job title is industrial machinery repairer, maintenance machinists, or industrial maintenance mechanic.

Maintenance and Repair Worker

This individual is the person who performs activities to keep machinery and equipment in good repair. Depending on the industry sector, these workers may be pipefitters, boilermakers, welders, or carpenters, in addition to electrical or machinery repair technicians. Maintenance and repair workers advance to have additional or supervisory responsibilities or, with additional training, to industrial machinery mechanics or electricians. Entry-level maintenance and repair workers have a high school diploma or GED. They may also be called general maintenance technicians or maintenance mechanics.

Maintenance Planner

A typical manufacturing plant has a tremendous amount of equipment and machinery to maintain. The maintenance planner schedules preventative maintenance and non-emergency repair work to ensure that all the machinery is kept in working order. He or she estimates and requisitions labor, parts, materials, tools, equipment, and any other resources needed for the maintenance or repair procedure. The planner coordinates with operations and production staff and the maintenance supervisor to get the work done.

Entry-level maintenance planners typically have a high school diploma or GED and experience in maintenance and repair work. Some companies prefer an associate's degree and experience. A few companies are looking for employees with a bachelor's degree in engineering or a related field.

Millwright

This is the individual who installs, replaces, and repairs machinery and heavy equipment. Advances in all areas of manufacturing mean that millwrights often work with highly complex or brand new machines, often specific to the industry sector they work in.

Millwrights work with production managers and industrial engineers to determine placement for machinery, and then may be
responsible for building the foundation and assembling the equipment. They work closely with industrial machinery mechanics and
maintenance and repair workers to take care of the equipment.
Millwrights may work night shifts.

Once on the job, millwrights take part in apprenticeship programs. Advancement typically means higher wages, but some may
advance to supervisory positions. Entry-level employees have a high
school diploma or GED and on the job training or experience.

Administration and Management

Like all companies, manufacturing establishments have employees who focus on management, finance, and administration. They
are not directly involved in creating or producing the final product.
Instead, these are the individuals who are responsible for the bigger picture. They develop and direct the strategic vision of the company, they organize employees and staff the company, they keep the
finances in order, or they lead and motivate the employees.

Accounting Manager

This is the person who takes care of the big picture in terms of
accounting and finance. They have standard accounting and finance
duties in addition to management and supervisory responsibilities.
They also ensure that departments and reporting meet all internal
audit standards. They often advance to controller, treasurer, or vice
president of finance.

Entry-level accounting managers have a bachelor's degree in
accounting and are certified public accountants. Some started out
their career as cost accountants. Most manufacturers want accounting managers with cost accounting experience.

Cost Accountant

At the most basic level, cost accountants look at the cost to run the
business, including costs for products, supplies, raw materials, and
labor. They work with budgets and inventory, ensure compliance
with cost standards, and create reports for management. Advancement is to accounting manager or budget director. Entry-level cost

accountants have a bachelor's degree in accounting. They may be certified public accountants, but not all companies require that. Many employers also look for experience in manufacturing.

Director of Operations

Operations is the part of the business where the day to day work gets done and the product gets made. The director of operations is the person with oversight of all the manufacturing operations. In addition, he or she sets policies, oversees the facilities, maintains quality in production and safety in operations, and is a leader for production and operations employees.

Operations director is a senior level position, reporting to the vice president of finance or operations or directly to the president or chief executive office. In some companies, operations directors may be a vice president level position. Advancement means a move up to the vice president level or beyond—to vice president of operations or finance, or to chief executive officer. Entry-level operations directors have a bachelor's or master's degree and at least ten years of experience in a manufacturing environment, such as plant manager. In addition to manufacturing experience, most companies expect operations directors to have senior management level experience.

Human Resource Manager

The human resource manager is the person who makes sure that a business has the right people working for it and that those employees do the work and receive the proper benefits for doing so. They recruit employees, provide training opportunities, manage employee benefits programs, ensure the company meets all employment regulations and laws, interact with employees and management, and in some companies manage union relations. In larger organizations, there may be human resource personnel or management staff devoted to each one of these tasks.

Human resource managers advance to human resource directors, which can be a vice president–level position, or to director of industrial relations. Entry-level human resource managers have a bachelor's degree in business or a human resources–related discipline, as well as experience in the field or a particular human resources specialty. Some manufacturers look for individual certified in areas like employee benefits or compensation.

Industrial Production Manager

This production manager is responsible for planning and coordinating all production activities in a manufacturing facility. The primary job may be creating and managing the production schedule, including which machines to use and when, whether new equipment is required, when to run the facility overtime, and ensuring that the entire process stays on schedule. As part of this role, industrial production managers must find ways to improve efficiency, often by introducing quality or production programs like Six Sigma or Total Quality Management. Some industrial production managers oversee an entire plant, and some are responsible for just one area. Depending on the size of the company, this individual may do a job that is similar to, or overlapping, that of the plant manager.

These individuals coordinate closely with management and other operations departments—finance, sales, procurement, production, and logistics. They report to the plant manager or vice president of manufacturing—those are the positions they may advance to, as well. Entry-level industrial production managers have a bachelor's degree in business, management, engineering, or industrial technology. Some may have a bachelor's degree in a liberal arts discipline combined with production experience, including starting out in production and advancing through supervisory and management positions. In addition, on the job training and certification in areas like production and inventory management help employees advance to this position.

Labor Relations Manager

Manufacturing establishments that work with unionized employees have labor relations managers to coordinate that relationship. They interpret and administer contracts and understand labor law and collective bargaining. As union membership declines, labor relations managers also work with non-union employees on labor and contract issues.

Advancement is to the director of industrial relations, or to the top management or executive level such as vice president of labor relations. Entry-level labor relations managers have a bachelor's degree in human resources, labor relations, or a related field. A master's degree or work in collective bargaining or labor law may be helpful for advancement. Some companies require labor relations managers to have a law degree.

Plant Manager

The plant manager is the individual responsible for operations and activities in the entire manufacturing facility. They work closely with sales, distribution, and health and safety and oversee all aspects of quality, production, scheduling, and safety. As managers, employees like manufacturing engineers report directly to plant managers. Depending on the size of the facility, the job of the plant manager may overlap with or be similar to that of industrial production manager. Often, this individual supervises the industrial production manager.

Advancement is to the vice president or executive level, such as director of operations or vice president of manufacturing. Plant managers usually have a bachelor's degree or equivalent amount of production or operations experience.

Regulatory Compliance Manager

Most manufacturing companies have at least a few government or industry regulations to adhere to. Some, like food production or pharmaceuticals, have a tremendous number of them. The job of the regulatory compliance manager is to manage the compliance program, ensure proper documentation, and work closely with the appropriate regulators.

Internally, they work closely with departments such as legal and human resources. In pharmaceutical companies, the regulatory compliance manager assists with submissions to the Food and Drug Administration. Entry-level regulatory compliance managers have a bachelor's degree in business, economics, accounting, or a related field. They also have experience in quality assurance or in a regulatory environment.

Sales Representative

No matter how wonderful or revolutionary a company's product may be, it is not anything until it is sold to a customer. That is where the sales representatives come in. It is their job to find customers, present the product to them, and negotiate the sale. They also must be able to answer technical questions about the product. In some companies, the sales representative may team with a sales engineer who will be able to address the scientific or technical features of the product.

Outside sales representatives work in the field, visiting customers at their facilities and offices. Most work from home and have sales territories, which may entail travel. Inside sales representatives sell products over the phone. They are available to answer questions and take orders. They typically work in the office and do not travel.

Sales representatives advance to purchasing or marketing positions, to sales trainers or supervisors, or simply by getting larger territories or accounts. Some representatives may be certified, but that is not necessary for advancement. Entry-level sales representatives may have bachelor's degrees, but a high school diploma or GED, job experience, and a strong desire to sell are all that is really required.

Technical Writer

Many manufactured goods require detailed instructions for construction or maintenance. Technical writers are the individuals who organize the materials and write or edit the documentation. The technical writer usually is not the subject matter expert, so he or she works with the engineers, management team, or customer representatives to get content and technical advice. Entry-level technical writers typically have a bachelor's degree and some experience in the industry.

Vice President of Manufacturing

In small manufacturing companies, this executive may be responsible for day to day supervisory tasks as well as purchasing and hiring responsibilities. In larger organizations, this person is more focused on the overall performance of manufacturing operations. Typically, this is the individual who oversees all plant operations like production scheduling, equipment purchasing and maintenance, staffing, research and development, and building and grounds.

Advancement is to president or chief executive officer of the company. In order to become a vice president of manufacturing, individuals must have strong leadership skills, significant management experience, and a strong record of accomplishments in manufacturing operations. In some companies, international experience or fluency in a second language may be required.

Chapter 4

Tips for Success

All sectors of manufacturing have been undergoing tremendous changes in the past several years: a shortage of qualified labor, improved productivity, challenging economic conditions, and a surge in global competition. Competition is fierce and profit margins are thin. This means that what businesses need from their employees has changed, too. As always, manufacturers need employees with basic skills—machining, processing, technology. But they also need employees who can solve problems, think critically, and be flexible—whether it is by cross training or by learning a new technology or machine.

News reports continue to focus on the loss of jobs, layoffs, and the movement of jobs overseas. Yet a great number of manufacturers complain of a lack of qualified, skilled labor. As the Baby Boom generation leaves the workforce, at least some of those employees will need to be replaced. As the work changes and becomes more technologically advanced, manufacturers will need workers with more technical skill and those who can work in what may look less and less like a traditional manufacturing environment.

Another reason behind the labor shortage is that younger people are not choosing manufacturing as a career. In addition, the widespread but outdated belief that the manufacturing business is all about machines and low pay drives away those who might otherwise be interested. Also, upcoming generations have ideas about job satisfaction and careers that can seem at odds with the way a manufacturing establishment works.

Manufacturers are working to adapt to new ways of working and to technological advances. They are also trying to help high school and college students learn about the reality of the industry today, hoping to expose them to the many opportunities available in the industry. Young people are not being trained for careers in manufacturing. So some manufacturers are working with business leaders and schools to create training programs and manufacturing-friendly curricula.

Taking Advantage of the Opportunities in Manufacturing

Manufacturers are having a hard time attracting qualified employees. So, while finding a job or advancing is not necessarily simple, opportunities are there for those willing to work hard. The turmoil in the industry means that there are fabulous opportunities for those who are willing to look for them.

If you already have a manufacturing job, now is the time to expand your knowledge of the industry or your specific job. Find out what education or training your employer offers and take it. It is easier and less expensive for employers to train existing employees than have to look outside for new talent, and that is to your benefit. When the economy is struggling, it is even more important that you keep up to date with changes in the industry and advances in technology. Consider taking outside classes or working toward a certification. This also may be the time for you to look for advancement opportunities—inside or outside your current company. When labor is short, those with proper skills, attitude, and experience rise to the top.

This is also a good time to share what you know with your employer. Anything that makes you stand out positively is a good thing. Do you have ideas for improving productivity? Saving your company money is always a good thing—your contribution will be noted. Do you have an idea for a recycling program or other way to help your company become green? In addition to being good for the environment and often productivity as well, environmental responsibility is also good public relations for any company. Make a name for yourself by helping improve your company's reputation. Share your ideas with your supervisor or someone who can make them happen, then help implement them. Make sure that your supervisor and upper management know it was your idea.

Another way to shine in your current company is to become an expert in something. These days, employees can make themselves indispensable by becoming the go-to person. Learn about a particular process in your facility, read everything about a particular aspect of the industry that intrigues you, or participate in an industry organization.

If you are not currently working in the manufacturing business, but want to make a career change, make sure that you can give employers what they are desperately searching for: someone with an understanding of technology and business, someone who can communicate effectively, someone who can make a strong contribution, and someone with a passion—for the job or the industry. Focus on your strengths and talents, and look at what skills you already have that are transferable to the new industry—such as communication skills, management experience, and technical skills.

If you have a strong desire, but are lacking in experience or education, a little training may be all you need. This may be through an apprenticeship or internship, or perhaps through a class at your local community college. Many have certificate or two-year programs that focus on particular areas of production and manufacturing. You may even be able to work in the industry while you are studying, and that will give you an advantage when you finish school.

Think about the size of the company you work in now, or want to be working in. There are advantages to working in firms of all sizes. If you work in a small firm, there will not be as many job openings. However, it can be easier to advance in a smaller company than in a larger one. Take advantage of cross training opportunities and develop as wide a range of skills as you can. In smaller firms, there is a smaller pool of employees looking to move up. You will likely work more closely with your supervisor and have more opportunity to differentiate yourself from your peers. Larger companies offer more jobs to choose from and usually a greater number of chances for advancement or lateral moves. But there may be more competition from other employees as well as outside candidates. It can also be a bit more difficult to make yourself stand out in the crowd in a larger organization.

Key Success Factors

There are several factors that go into succeeding as an employee at a manufacturing firm, no matter your role or level in an organization. In all areas of a company, employers value good communication

Keeping in Touch

A Professional Online Reputation

- Join professional networking sites like LinkedIn and post information about your experience, your strengths, and your career goals.

- On personal networking sites like Facebook, the best bet is to make your profile private. If you want your profile to be public, do not post pictures or stories you wouldn't want your grandmother to see, or anything you wouldn't want an employer to know about you.

- On occasion, some people recommend at least once a week, search for yourself online and see what information is posted about you.

- If the information is not what you want, you have got two choices: add more relevant information to the Web or ask the content owner to remove it. If you cannot get something removed, at least you can push it farther down the results list by adding relevant content. Comment on key industry Web sites, publish articles online, join professional or industry networking sites, or develop a Web page with your professional portfolio.

skills, timeliness, collaboration, and teamwork. They value employees who are willing to take on new challenges, especially ones that are unpleasant and that no one else wants to do. They also value employees who can gracefully accept credit for success as well as responsibility for making a mistake.

Take Control of Your Manufacturing Career

Years ago, it may have been standard practice to start working in one company and stay there for your whole career. Career paths were pretty well mapped out, and employers helped you along the way. That is no longer the case. It can happen, but it is unusual now for someone to spend his or her whole career in one company. For many people, it is unusual to spend an entire career in one industry. Today it is much more common to switch companies after a few years in order to advance up the ranks and expand experience.

These days, employers are not as hands-on with managing their employees' career paths. Although many companies will offer some form of guidance, employees are expected to manage their own training, skills, advancement, and career path. If you want training or more responsibility, you may have to ask for it. You need to be hungry and proactive.

Balance Your Work Life and Personal Life

Hard work and focus are important. But giving yourself over to the job is not. There are jobs that require overtime or longer hours on occasions like peak production times or toward the quarter- or year-end. In many jobs, though, staying late is not always a sign of success. Sometimes it means that you couldn't finish your work during the time allotted. Make sure to take time for yourself, and get a break. Keep normal work hours when possible, take sick time when you are sick, and use up all your vacation time. Making sure you get enough rest and time off will increase your personal productivity in many ways.

Define What You Mean by Success

In the end, that is the most important step in having a successful career in manufacturing. Each person defines success differently, and each follows a different path to get there. If you do not know how you define success, you will not know when you get there. This does not necessarily have to be something formal, like a document on which you state your goals and the steps you take to reach them. It can be if you want it to be. But defining success can simply mean understanding what you want out of your working life.

It is important that it be your own goal. Success for some is a steady job with decent pay and never having to work overtime. For others, it is advancement from an inventory job to a management position. Someone else may consider himself successful if he gets a degree or certification that moves him up a pay grade. Another may consider herself successful only if she becomes a vice president or director.

There usually are many paths to reach your ultimate goal. More and more these days, promotions and advancement do not take a linear path. Getting additional training or education in one area, like quality control for example, may lead to opportunities in production or management. Be willing to be creative and have fun on your way to your goal. Work is work, so it will not always be fun or rewarding. But when you are doing something you really enjoy—working in a field you like, or sharing your day with a team of people you treasure—it does make work feel less like work.

Succeeding in Manufacturing Management

Management level jobs require different skills than those needed on the production floor or front lines. The most important skill to have as a manager is to be able to work well with others. Managers act as a liaison between the executive level and the production floor. That means both good communication skills and the ability to build rapport and trust are important. Managers need to communicate effectively with production and operations staff—to push information down to the employees who report directly to them and the employees on the levels below. Managers need to be able to share company policies and strategic direction, assign job tasks and responsibilities, discuss day-to-day operations and issues, and review and discuss job performance.

Managers also need to communicate effectively with executives and management. They need to be able to share with them operational challenges, activities, or events that may impact the company's strategic direction, and issues with employees or the facilities. Managers need to be able to communicate verbally—they may be asked to give presentations, for example, and they need to be able to write well. Management jobs require report writing, such as quality or inventory reports, in addition to daily communications like email and memos, which are important for corresponding internally with employees and management and externally with customers and suppliers.

Managers are leaders. Part of leading any group of people, no matter the size, is understanding the group dynamics. Find out which skills employees have and helping them use those skills to their best advantage. Although each person is responsible for his or her own career, to a certain degree employees put part of their career success in the hands of their supervisors and managers. It is important in your dealings with those who report to you to be honest, straightforward, and fair. When you get down to it, a good leader wants individual employees to shine and the team to succeed.

An understanding of the company and industry is another skill that supervisory and management employees need to have in order to succeed. They also need to have a clear picture of how their department and employees contribute to the overall success of the company. Managers are expected to take care of day-to-day operations, but also must be able to contribute to the overall business strategy and see the big picture. The higher up the management track you are, the more important it is to know not only about your company, but about the industry sector as well. Relationships with customers, colleagues in other companies, and professional organizations help you gain this knowledge, as well as indicate your commitment.

Succeeding in Production and Operations

Production and operations jobs are all about producing things and keeping the process working smoothly. Manual dexterity, mechanical aptitude, good vision, and the ability to lift and move objects are important basic skills for most of these jobs. In addition, good communication and interpersonal skills are vital. Assemblers and others who work in teams need to communicate with the team, and all employees need to be able to effectively communicate with their managers or supervisors.

Flexibility is another skill that production and operations employees need. Technology improvements can mean new equipment and machinery, or a change in the way work is performed. Employees are expected to adapt to these changes quickly, so productivity and operational efficiency are not affected. Hand in hand with this type of flexibility is an eagerness to learn and continuously improve. Whether due to new processes, new equipment, new technologies, or new management initiatives, on-the-job training is a fact of life in a manufacturing facility. Employees who embrace this have a better chance of success.

Companies place great importance on quality, so employees need to be accurate and have strong attention to detail. Employees at all levels are expected to identify defects and mistakes, and make the appropriate adjustments for improvement. This skill is especially important for production employees who are hands-on with the materials and products.

Your Manufacturing Career Path

The traditional career path in a manufacturing establishment is a pretty straight line up the chain of command. From production and operations jobs, to supervisory roles or department heads, to management positions, to the executive suite. However, there are now many paths that lead to advancement, often by adding on-the-job training or additional education. In general, advancement comes from taking on and successfully performing additional tasks or responsibilities, or taking on projects or responsibilities above your current work level.

Not all career paths have to lead to management. That is not something everyone wants or needs to do. Many career paths involve lateral moves, which do not necessarily indicate a deviation from the path. A lateral move can lead to more responsibility, higher salary, or better benefits, depending on the company and the new responsibilities you take on. You can stay in your general area of expertise—say production, or move to a different department using your production experience as a basis for a career in quality assurance.

Have a Plan

The important thing about planning your career path is the plan. When you know where you want to go, it is much easier to get there. You may not want to move all the way up into management, but that does not mean you do not want to get promoted, get more responsibilities, or make more money.

In some areas of production or operations, a promotion may include an increase in responsibilities and salary, but no management or supervisory responsibilities. To move into management from a more technical job is not as hard as it may seem. Technical expertise is increasingly in demand at the management level. In manufacturing jobs in particular, an understanding of production processes, product development, and inventory management is critical for understanding the business itself. It is crucial for management and executive level positions.

Take Charge

Advancement very often means taking charge of other employees. The best way to demonstrate your ability to manage other people is to manage yourself and your time. Then show ability to coach and motivate others, as well as being comfortable assigning work and holding others responsible. As you move up on a management track, you may be responsible for people more than one level below you, people who do not report directly to you. That means you must be an effective team member and leader, a great communicator, and you must be able to understand the jobs of all the employees and departments you are responsible for, even if you do not have direct experience in those jobs.

To move beyond effective management, you need to have a sense of what the business needs and where you and your department or

Best Practice

Interview Etiquette

Show up on time. In fact, plan to arrive early. It is better to spend a little time sitting in your car, walking around the building, or sitting in the reception area than arriving rushed and flustered or worse—late.

Be prepared. Do some research into the industry, company, or executive before you arrive, have your notes handy, and write out any specific questions you want answered.

Turn off your cell phone and put it away. At the very least, turn the ringer off, do not answer or place any calls or text messages, and do not check it during the interview. Your focus is on the interview and the interviewer.

Dress for success. A suit is best, but if you do not have one a dressy pair of pants and shirt, or dress or nice skirt and top are best. Do not be casual. That means no shorts, flip-flops, tank tops, jeans, or the like. It is better to be overdressed than appear too casual.

Send a thank you note to everyone you interviewed with and to anyone who helped you out, like the receptionist or staff assistant. A hand written note is best, but an email thank you note is better than nothing.

direct reports fit into it. Moving up to supervisor or management positions usually means having to think strategically about the business and how your department contributes to the company's profits—not just about the particulars of your job.

Stretch Yourself

Be a problem solver and stretch yourself. That is how you get more experience on the job. Take on a project that feels beyond your current skill level or offer to help your manager with a task a level or two above your typical responsibilities. Volunteer for challenging assignments outside your comfort zone. Continue your education, whether that means getting a degree or certification or taking advantage of on-the-job training available to you.

Be Seen

The other thing about advancing your career involves personal public relations. Your supervisor does not know about your goals unless you tell him or her about them. When you make your performance plan for the year, talk about your goals at the company or in the industry—short and long term. In addition to sharing your thoughts with your boss, get his or her support in your quest. No matter how hard you work, you will not get far without it.

Also, make sure to network with your colleagues and consider finding a mentor. Sometimes the next best step is just finding a better job in-house and applying for it. Get to know the people and processes in other departments, especially any that you wish to become part of. Keep on top of what is going on with internal job postings and keep an eye out for them.

Education and On-the-job Training

If you have a high school diploma or a GED, you can get many types of jobs in a manufacturing facility, such as model maker, assembler, shipping clerk, or machinist. On-the-job training in the company's processes, machinery, or advanced assembly and finishing, or taking classes at a vocational school or community college, will help you advance to the next level, such as to a machinist or welder.

If you have an associate's degree, you can get a job such as technologist or semiconductor technician. On-the-job training or continuing

Fast Facts

Questions Employers Cannot Ask

You will get asked all sorts of questions in a job interview. But there are a few that employers are legally prohibited from asking. They cannot ask:

- Are you a U.S. citizen? They can ask if you are legally authorized to work in the United States.

- What is your religion? They can ask you which days you are able to work.

- How old are you? They can ask if you are over the age of 18.

- Do you have children? They can ask if your schedule allows you to travel or work overtime.

- Are you pregnant or do you plan to have kids? They can ask about your long-term career plans.

- Do you have any disabilities? They can ask if you will be able to perform the specific duties of the specific job.

- The U.S. Equal Employment Opportunity Commission (http://www.eeoc.gov) has information on federal laws and facts and guidance about discriminatory practices by type (age, disability, national origin, etc.).

education from a local community college or career school will help you advance to the next level. If you have a bachelor's degree, you can get a job as an engineer, a production manager, or executive. On-the-job training or an advanced degree may help you advance to the next level, although an additional degree is not always necessary. If you have a master's degree, you can get a job as a researcher, engineer, or an executive. Experience and industry knowledge are typically the ways to advance up to the top executive level.

Apprenticeship

Apprenticeship is an age-old tradition of a student learning a trade from a skilled employer. In manufacturing, it is a way to combine formal and classroom instruction with a mentor and standardized on-the-job training. Apprentices are usually paid a small wage during the course of training. In many cases, the coursework is done at a two- or four-year college and counts toward an associate's or bachelor's degree. Apprenticeships are voluntary programs offered by individual companies, unions, or other organizations.

These organizations work in conjunction with the U.S. Department of Labor Office of Apprenticeship, which sets program standards including how apprentice are paid, the amount of supervision, and the measurement of the apprentice's progress. For example, the National Institute for Metalworking Skills requires specific competencies for each apprenticeship. A certified mold maker must be able to perform many tasks, including surface grinding, CNC basic programming, and part inspection, as well as be able to explain metallurgical theory and sensor function.

In 2007, some of the top 25 apprenticeship occupations were manufacturing related: electrician, heavy truck driver, sheet metal worker, operating engineer, and millwright. There were more than 16,000 apprentices in the manufacturing industry. There are apprenticeships for individuals who work in one of many manufacturing sectors, such as tool and die makers, machinists, and mechanics. However, individual industry sectors may have their own apprenticeship programs. The aerospace sector, for example, has registered apprenticeships for aircraft structures assemblers and aircraft inspectors.

Certification

Certification is formal documentation by a third party that an individual is competent in a set of qualifications or performance standards. This requires an assessment process such as an examination, demonstration of a capability, or records of relevant work-related experience. Getting certified is voluntary and is a way for employees to document their skills and experience.

A logistics specialist, for example, may seek certification in transportation and logistics from the American Society of Transportation and Logistics. To become certified, she must successfully complete exams in the areas of general management, transportation economics, logistics, international transport and logistics, and two elective subjects.

A purchasing manager may work with the Institute of Supply Management to become a certified purchasing manager. He would need to successfully complete exams in purchasing process, supply environment, value enhancement strategies, and management.

If you are pursuing a certification to help with advancement or for another reason, talk with your employer to understand which certifications they accept and how they will support you as you pursue certification. Employers do not offer certifications—industry groups or third-party organizations provide evidence of certification.

Community Colleges

Studying manufacturing related topics at a community college is open to anyone with a high school degree or GED. Employees with bachelor's degrees may take a course or attend a community college program in order to update work skills. States have many community colleges that offer programs in manufacturing jobs such as machinist, electrical and electronic engineering technician, logistics, biotechnology lab technician, welding, chemical technology, environmental science, and avionics technicians.

If you currently work in manufacturing and want to update your skills, check with your employer to see which programs they recommend for the position you are in or want to advance to. Also, find out if they will pay for all or part of your schooling. Many companies have tuition reimbursement programs for employees who take courses or pursue a degree related to their job.

Internships

Internships offer individuals a chance to get experience doing a job, to meet individuals in the industry, and to learn the ropes. Internships are offered by individual companies. In large companies, they are often formal programs. In some companies, typically smaller ones, they may be less formal and give the individual more latitude for structuring the experience. Many internships are unpaid or offer college credit instead of payment, making them ideal for college students and recent graduates. Some programs are part-time. All internships, though, are offered for a set period of time—a semester, a summer, or six months, for example. Think hard before accepting an internship, especially an unpaid one, as they are not the right option for everyone.

If pursuing an internship is something you can and want to do, however, it is a great way to learn about a particular occupation and industry. That is especially true if you are just starting out in your career and are not sure which type of job interests you the most. It is also a great way to learn about the job search process, as applying to an internship is exactly like applying for a full-time job. As an added benefit to all that work, in many cases interns apply for and get full-time jobs in the same company they interned with. They know the job, the company, and the people who work there—and the people who work there know them.

Vocational School

Like community colleges, vocational or career schools enable individuals to get additional training without having to pursue a four-year college degree program. You can study in areas such as assembling, computer technologies, inspection, machining, and welding.

As with other educational opportunities, work with your employer to find out if a specific vocational program will help your career, perhaps by providing training that is not available in-house at the company or through a local community college. Work with your supervisor or human resources professional to determine the best choice of courses or programs for your career, and find out if they will help with the tuition. Many companies help their employees pay for additional training via a vocational or career school, especially if it is training that is difficult to get on the job or for them to offer in-house.

The educational opportunities discussed above are also available to an individual who is not yet working in the manufacturing industry. They are a great way to learn a skill or get valuable training or on-the-job experience. If that is the case, ask the school about the graduates of the program. Ask about which companies have hired graduates and what kinds of jobs they have been able to get. Ask to speak to a couple graduates in the program you are considering. Check with the local Better Business Bureau to make sure there haven't been any complaints. Before spending money and investing your time in taking classes and pursuing a degree or certification, make sure you will get the training and knowledge you are looking for and that you will be able to use the qualification in the job, company, or industry sector you are targeting.

How to Find a Manufacturing Job

If you want to get into manufacturing, but do not know exactly what sector you want to work in or what job you would like, there are a few tools to help you figure out what you want to do. These tools will help you identify where your passions lie and what type of manufacturing job will suit your personality.

Dream It. Do It. The National Association of Manufacturers Manufacturing Institute joined with the American Association of Community Colleges, the College Board, and Monster.com to create a Web site (http://www.dreamit-doit.com) to help encourage people to pursue manufacturing careers. It has a job search function and a career quiz that will help identify your strengths and where you fit in a manufacturing company.

What Color is Your Parachute? By Richard Bolles (2009). This classic career guide is updated annually and has been helping people find their passion for over 30 years. It is a great place to start if you need guidance in finding out what you truly enjoy doing and how to turn that into a career. The Web site (http://www.jobhuntersbible.com) has many useful articles and links to online career tests and other job-hunting resources.

Now, Discover Your Strengths. By Marcus Buckingham and Donald O. Clifton (2001). Almost everyone can be trained to do certain job-related tasks. But the fact is that most people have a few areas they excel in, and the rest they are basically competent in. This book helps individuals find their talents and strengths, and then to build on those strengths to find the best career for each individual.

Networking

Networking and meeting new people is a critical step in finding a job. It is especially important if you are new to the industry or a particular sector of the industry. One of the tricky things about networking is that you need to be doing it before you need to capitalize on it—and that is usually the time no one ever feels like doing it. Networking is not about asking someone for a job or a favor. It is about building relationships. So if you haven't been networking yet, now is the time to start.

The best way to start networking is with people you know—friends, neighbors, relatives, teachers, and former colleagues. Share with them what kind of job you are looking for, the industry sector that interests you, the skills you want to use, the responsibilities you want to have. You never know who has a friend, neighbor, or in-law working in the industry.

Meet New People
After you have let everyone in your circle know about you quest, it is time to start meeting new people. Go to events such as school or employee alumni events, industry conferences and conventions, or chamber of commerce events. Use business online networking sites like LinkedIn or personal networking sites like Facebook. Online sites are a great way to identify connections—you get to see who is connected to the people you know. Then you can ask your contact for an introduction to their connection, either online or in person. One thing to keep in mind: Online networking is great, but should not be a substitute for meeting people in person.

Speaking of online networking, it is important to keep your online reputation as clean and professional as possible. Among other things, potential employers do online searches to learn about you. Search results typically include your profiles on sites like LinkedIn or Facebook, blog posts and comments, and personal Web sites. Potential employers use this information to get a sense of who you are before they even meet you. There are cases of employers rejecting candidates because of unacceptable information found on the Internet.

Tell Your Story
Although much of networking is about listening to find out how you can help others, you will need to talk about yourself. When you attend an event or meet someone, you should be prepared. Plan an elevator speech—a 20 to 30 second speech that talks about who you are, what you do, and what you are looking for. There is a lot of advice about exactly what someone should say in that elevator speech. Some people recommend that it be enigmatic, to prompt questions. Others suggest it be simple and straightforward. Still others suggest finding out who you are talking to first then tailoring what you say to who they are. In the end, there are only two things that matter in an elevator speech: That you are comfortable saying it, and that it imparts the information you wish to share. Also, make sure to bring business cards to give to people you talk to. It is the easiest way to share information and, if you do not have any or do

not want to use business cards from your current company, it is easy and inexpensive to have some made up.

Have a Plan

Like so many things in a job search, networking works better when you have a plan. Very few people are natural networkers. Most people are quite shy about it. Those who do well at networking do so because they have a plan. When you know you will be attending a party, event, or conference there are a couple of things to think about. First, think about who you want to meet—either individuals by name, or people who work in a particular company or industry. Many organizations hand out attendee lists prior to the event or at the door.

Next, think about what you want to accomplish at the event. Do you want to meet five new people? Do you want to identify and introduce yourself to people in a particular company or industry sector? Then, think about what you want to walk out of the room with, such as business cards, plans to meet for coffee, or a new LinkedIn contact. Lastly, after the event is over, follow up with the people that you met. Write a short thank you note, and make a plan to meet or just to keep in touch.

Networking, whether online or in person, is about being available to your contacts. Be ready to help out your new friends and acquaintances. Introduce them to your contacts or answer a question for them. That is how you build relationships with the people that you meet, and that is how you become a better networker.

Cover Letters

The goal of a cover letter is to get the human resources professional or, ideally, the hiring manager to read your résumé. It should discuss the particular job you are applying for and explain why you are the right person for it. It needs to be tailored to the job you are applying for and addressed to a specific person by name.

Use the letter to sell yourself and convince the hiring manager that you can help him or her. Do research into the industry, the company, and the specific job so you can identify keywords to use, important skills to highlight, and how you will add the most value to the company. This is where the posted job description and research into the company come in handy. Think of this as a marketing piece about yourself, showing off what you know about the job and the industry.

Your Résumé

While the goal of the cover letter is to get someone to read your résumé, the goal of your résumé is to get invited in for an interview. It is a snapshot of your education, experience, and accomplishments. Tailor your résumé to the job you are applying for, highlighting the specific skills and job responsibilities the employer is looking for. If you are applying for an existing job, look at the job description. Employers will tell you exactly what they are seeking in a job applicant. Highlight relevant experience, education, and training that fit the needs of the job you are applying for. Make sure to use industry-standard terms and keywords. If you have experience working with a particular machine, for example, use the generic or standard term for that machine, not the brand name or any company-specific names used by your previous company.

When you apply for jobs with different requirements, you will need to create different versions of your résumé for each. If you are writing your résumé for posting on a career site, it may have to be more general. In this case, still make sure to include keywords related to the job requirements and the industry sector. Because of the number of résumés employers receive directly or review on job search sites, they have a few tricks to weed through them. Many use applicant tracking systems that search for keywords in the content of the résumé and cover letter, such as specific skills or experience, and they will not look at résumés or cover letters do not meet those requirements.

Remember that whether you post it online or submit it directly to an employer when applying for an open position, your résumé must represent you to someone who has never met you.

A few things to think about as you pull together the content:

→ What do you want to accomplish? What is the job or responsibility you are seeking?

→ What are your relevant skills? Think about computer programs you use, languages you speak, machines you know how to operate, or other industry-specific skills.

→ What have you accomplished—in your schooling or career? These should be specific, quantifiable things beyond your job responsibilities, such as promotions, awards, certifications, licenses, or special projects you have completed successfully.

➡ What is your professional experience and specific job responsibilities? When you are applying in a specific industry or for a particular job, make sure to include and highlight experiences and responsibilities that are relevant to typical jobs tasks or the industry.

One final point about résumés and cover letters: they need to be perfect. Spelling or grammar mistakes indicate a lack of attention and many human resource professionals or hiring managers will simply move on to the next résumé when they discover an error like that.

For advice on writing your résumé and cover letter, visit job search sites like ManufacturingJobs.com, Monster.com, or Career-Launcher.com, or go to the library or career center and look through career books like *What Color is Your Parachute?* or *Knock 'Em Dead: The Ultimate Job Search Guide*. These resources offer specific advice and recommendations about to highlight your skills and experience and correctly format your résumé and cover letter.

Interviews

There are two types of interviews you may find yourself on during a job search. Each has a different purpose.

Informational Interview

An informational interview is time you request to speak with someone in the industry, often a friend or a colleague of a friend. In addition to expanding your network, an informational interview is your chance to learn from industry insiders and to ask questions about a specific type of job and what is expected from someone in that role, about the industry itself, or about qualifications for different types of jobs. If you do not have a lot of practice at job interviews, informational interviews are great practice and a way to get interview experience without the stress of having a job on the line.

Informational interviews help you learn all sorts of things about an industry. That is a huge benefit if you are a career changer or new to the working world. You will start to learn the industry vocabulary, what jobs, career paths, typical days in the industry are like. You might also identify specific companies you may be interested in working for.

There are two ways to identify prospects for informational interviews: cold calls and personal connections. Although cold calling can feel difficult, if you do not have any connections in the industry this is the best way to make contact. Whichever way you make the initial contact, it is natural to feel nervous. Remember one thing: People who agree to help you with an informational interview want to help you succeed.

When you make contact to request the interview, use your best professional written or spoken voice. Tell them who you are and how you got their name—through a friend or colleague, or from their involvement in an industry organization, for example. Tell them what you are interested in learning—for example, that you want to learn about production jobs in the medical device industry because of your interests in engineering and medicine; or that you want to learn about the beverage processing industry to see where you might fit in. Ask for the time to sit down with them for this interview—no more than 30 minutes.

When you arrive for the interview, remember the reason you are there: to get information and learn about the industry. You are not there to ask for a job. Keep the interview focused and on time. And never, ever go over the time you have asked for unless the person you are meeting specifically asks you to.

Arrive prepared. Before setting up the interview, you will have done research into the industry and the company. Bring a list of questions to ask, and take notes during the interview. Despite doing research, you may have missed a key aspect of the industry. Be ready to ask different questions and follow the conversation it if takes you down an interesting or important path.

Although you are there to learn about the industry or the company, an informational interview is also a great chance to ask specific questions about your situation. If you are lacking what you think is a key skill or educational requirement, for example, ask about it. Find out if a skill or degree is a requirement for the kind of work you are looking for, or if it is just something that employers prefer and if there are ways to work around it. Talk a little bit about what interests you. When you are talking to an industry insider, they can help you understand if your interests and passions are a fit with the industry or the type of job you are considering.

Start wrapping up before your time has elapsed. Ask for names of other people that you can speak to about the topic, and confirm if you can use your contact's name when making that connection. This is a great way to build your network.

Informational interviews typically take place in the office of the person you are interviewing. As they are taking time out of their work day to speak with you, it is best for you to go to his or her office. On rare occasions, it may make sense to meet outside of the work environment, but do not suggest that yourself. One benefit of visiting the person in his or her office is to see what it looks like. If there is a production facility at the office location, you may even get a tour. However, unless you requested a tour in advance or it is explicitly offered to you, do not expect or ask for one while you are there for the interview.

Although you should not expect the interview to be anything other than a chance for you to get information from someone in the industry, sometimes an informational interview will become the basis for a job interview and eventually a job. It is important that you treat the interview as a key part of the process and extend all the same courtesies as you would on a job interview.

Job Interview

A job interview happens when an employer thinks you are qualified for a specific job and wants to talk to you in person. This is when you have to really prepare. Before you go in, make sure you have done research into the requirements of the specific job. If you cannot get too much information from the company Web site or the job description, do research into similar companies—they will often have similar job roles and titles. Ask friends in the company or industry about the position. When you walk into the interview, you want to know as much about the job and the company as possible.

Job interviews can take a few different forms. Sometimes, the human resources department conducts the first level of interviews. Other times you may interview directly with the hiring manager. Sometimes, they may set up multiple interviews—with the manager, colleagues, and people who currently do the job. A panel of people may interview you, although this is usually more common for upper management positions. When they call to set up the interview, ask for as much information about the set-up as possible, so you can be prepared. If you are interviewing with several people over the span of a few hours, ask for at least one break in the middle of the process. They are not trying to wear you out, so take a moment to get a drink of water or stretch, and take a quick mental break.

On the Cutting

Edge

Finding a Job with Twitter

This social media tool limits its users to 140 characters per post, called a tweet, but that does not seem to limit its uses. Job seekers are using this new tool as part of their job search strategies. Here's how. Be proactive:

- Link to your online résumé or biography
- Use Twitter to establish yourself as an expert and build a following
- Tweet about your job search

Or use one of the following tools to be notified about or search for posted jobs:

- http://www.getmanufacturingjobs.com
- http://twitter.com.getmanufactjobs
- http://twitter.com/microjobs
- TweetMyJobs Get instant notification when the type of job you are seeking is posted: http://twitter.com/tweetmyjobs or http://tweetmyjobs.com
- TwitterJobSearch Search for Twitter job postings. Can search by title and location: http://www.twitterjobsearch.com
- @simplyhired Twitter version of the general job search site: http://www.simplyhired.com http://twitter.com/simplyhired

This tool changes fast. Keep your eyes open for more job posting and searching functions and other ways to exploit this tool as you look for a job.

Interviewing people for jobs is something that human resource managers have training for, but is not necessarily something that everyone you interview with will have experience with. So you may be asked all sorts of questions, with varying levels of expertise. Each person who interviews you will have questions specific to his or her role in the process. When you interview with a potential colleague, for example, they will want to know that you can do the job, but they will also want to know what it will be like to work with you every day.

In general, when you are asked in for a job interview, the employer already knows that you are qualified for the job. So the purpose is not to find out that you know how to work a certain machine or that you have experience with a certain software program. It is to get to know you and to get a feel for how you will fit with the company and its culture, how you will work with current employees and management, and whether you will succeed. Expect questions about your strengths and any weaknesses, about how you have dealt with certain types of work situations in the past, and why you think this type of work or this company would suit you. Also, expect questions that address any weaknesses, real or perceived, in your background and experience. If the job requires a bachelor's degree but you have an associate's degree and five years of experience, you may be asked to explain how you are, in fact, qualified for the job.

Remember that the interview works both ways. Although the bulk of it is someone asking you questions and you answering, you should ask questions, too. This is your chance to see if the company and its culture fit with who you are, if the management style and other employees seem like people you can work with, and for you to get a feel for whether this will be the right next step in your career.

Think about what is important to you in a work relationship. For example, a company may offer training opportunities that you may want to take advantage of, but perhaps they are only offered at certain times of the year or to employees with a specific job grade or years of experience. Ask about overtime—if it is expected for your role and if it is common. On paper you may be able to leave every day at 5:30, but no one ever walks about the door before 6:30. Ask about vacation time. While many companies offer a standard amount of vacation time, in some companies certain employees cannot take vacation any time they want. For example, production workers may have to be available at certain times in the cycle; finance workers may have to be available at the end of the fiscal quarters or end of the year.

This is not easy to do, but try to be relaxed. This may be your first job interview ever, or the only one you have been able to line up for two months, or you may really, really need this job. Your potential employer does not need to know this. The more you put those things out of your mind, the more relaxed you will be and the more like yourself you will be—and that is who your potential employer wants to meet.

Job Search Web Sites

There are a number of general job search sites that include manufacturing jobs. In most, you simply search by job title or by industry. There are also a few manufacturing-specific sites, some focused on a particular industry or aspect of an industry. Below is a sampling of job search sites that provide listings in the manufacturing industry or within specific industry sectors. Many organizations have industry-specific job listings available to members and nonmembers alike, so check out any relevant industry or trade associations, as well.

In addition to searching job aggregator sites, most manufacturers post job openings on their own Web sites. They often allow you to apply online by filling out a form and submitting your résumé. If you have a short list of companies you want to work for, searching their sites may be a better way than using job aggregator sites like those below. For the most part, jobs appear on a company's Web site before or at the same time they appear on an aggregator site.

BlueCollarJobs   Part of the Beyond.com network of niche career search sites. Can search jobs without registering, must register to apply online. Free registration and résumé uploading; links to manufacturing-specific communities. (http://www.bluecollar jobs.com)

CareerBuilder   General job search site, including jobs in all sectors of manufacturing. Can search jobs without registering. (http://www.careerbuilder.com)

Careers in Food   Food and beverage manufacturing jobs. Can search for jobs without registering; can apply to jobs without registering on the site—it offers links to employers' online application sites. Free registration. (http://www.careersinfood.com)

Dream It. Do It.   Run by the National Association of Manufacturers and Monster.com, this site is geared to young adults look for jobs in manufacturing. Can search for jobs without registering; can apply to jobs without registering on the site—it offers links to employers' online application sites. Free registration. (http://www.dreamit-doit.com)

IHireJobNetwork   Free registration and résumé uploading; users must be registered to search for jobs. Includes iHireManufacturingEngineers.com, iHireEngineering.com, iHireLogistics.com, iHireManufacturing.com, and iHireQualityControl.com.

INTERVIEW

Putting People First

Albert J. Weatherhead
Chairman and CEO, Weatherhead Industries

What is the most important quality for someone interested in working in the manufacturing industry?
The ability to understand and work with people. To me, it is always about what people are thinking, how they are reacting, their temperament. About relationships. Anyone can build a factory and put machinery in it. Unless you put the human qualities of kindness and spirit into it, it will not work as a business. For managers, it is important to understand the feelings of the people who work in the factory, understand their experience working where they do.

What do you look for in a prospective employee?
I look for someone who is honest and really wants to work. Someone who wants to contribute. Someone who wants to improve what is going on. Who will look at a process and have an idea for improvement. Someone who's willing to throw out the old way of doing things and do it another way if it is a better way. Someone who is flexible to make changes and learn.

What is the type of behavior that has caused you to fire someone?
We had a guy once who lasted just 17 days on the job. He came in and wanted to fire all of our superintendents and replace them with people he knew, his friends. The people he wanted to fire had been around a long time and were highly respected by their compatriots and peers. He wanted to disrupt a labor force of over 500 people. That was a good reason to fire him. And it took us a long time to recover from that. In another case, someone got so angry with me for trying

Jobs in Logistics Free registration and résumé uploading. Can search for jobs without registering; can apply to jobs without registering, although registering is best. (http://www.jobsinlogistics.com)

ManufacturingJobs Can search jobs without registering; can apply to jobs without registering on the site—it offers links to to improve a process he picked up the base plate for the mold we were working on and almost hit me with it. That was also a good reason to fire someone.

What are some mistakes you have made in your career that you'd like to help others avoid?

You want to make mistakes. That is the one thing in life you want to do. The minute you find you created an error, correct it right away. As fast as you can. If you do not make any mistakes, you do not expand your learning capabilities. It is part of growing up. We weren't born with this accumulated knowledge. Making mistakes educates you. And you educate yourself, so you know how to think.

In terms of trying to address challenges, I write things down. If I do not like it, I wad it up and throw it away. Sometimes you have to spend time studying something. And if you try to change something and it does not work, jumping ship might not be the solution. You cannot hide from your adversities. Because adversity is just a lovely wall to leap over.

What advice do you give people in the industry who are looking to move up the ladder?

I can tell by actions and attitudes that someone wants to improve. That is how I know if they should be brought along and given more responsibility little by little. Experience does not necessarily count for everything. Someone should have the ability to say no when they believe it is the wrong thing to do, even if they have to get a little rough about it. Individuals should spend time educating themselves, learning to think.

Some of my rules for mastering adversity are appropriate for individuals who are looking for advancement in the industry: Positive thinking is imperative. Cultivate the seven selfish virtues: modesty, gratitude, courtesy, self-control, compassion, perseverance, and indomitable spirit to conquer your adversity. Adversity always grants a chance to creatively resolve the problem. There is always a great idea lurking in adversity... Will you find it?

employers' online application sites. Free registration and résumé uploading. (http://www.manufacturingjobs.com)

Monster   General job search site, includes jobs in all sectors of manufacturing. Can search without registering; must register to apply online. (http://www.monster.com)

PharmaConnection   Pharmaceutical jobs. Can search without registering. Can apply to jobs without registering on the site—it offers links to employers' online application sites. Free registration and résumé uploading. (http://jobs.pharmamanufacturing .com)

Society of Manufacturing Engineers Jobs Connection   Can search for jobs without registering; can apply to jobs without registering on the site—it offers links to employers' online application sites. Free registration. (http://jobsconnection.sme.org)

Other Resources

Career Voyages   Government site run by Department of Labor and the Department of Education. Includes information about careers in manufacturing and other in-demand occupations. Provides information on finding apprenticeships, certifications, community college programs, and four-year college programs. (http:// www.careervoyages.gov)

U.S. Department of Labor Employment and Training Division Office of Apprenticeship   This site provide information about apprenticeships for individuals and employers. Includes links to national, regional, and state apprenticeship agencies. (http://www.doleta.gov/oa)

Chapter 5

Talk Like a Pro

active supplier   A supplier from whom a business has purchased goods, materials, or services in the last two years.

activity based costing   In cost accounting, a way of allocating costs to specific activities, customers, or projects. It helps manufacturers understand the relationship between resources and activities.

actual cost   Overhead costs such as labor and materials. It is a way of allocating the costs of the production process to a particular job.

aeration   The introduction of a gas into a liquid.

agile manufacturing   A way of producing products that enables manufacturers to rapidly respond to changing market conditions, customer needs, or changing technological developments. This sometimes means reconfiguring operations or relationships with suppliers or partners.

agitation   Manufacturing process of stirring or mixing; a term often applicable in food or chemical processes.

agribusiness   The business of producing and distributing agricultural goods and services. The term encompasses the entire supply chain: producers and manufacturers in food and fiber processing, fertilizer and farm equipment makers, wholesalers, distributors and transportation providers, and retail food and fiber establishments.

allocations   The actual demand for inventory, based on orders. This shows the level of demand.

alloy Material consisting of metal mixed with other metals or non-metals. Alloys are created to take advantage of specific properties of each of the component materials.

amalgam An alloy that includes one or more metals mixed with mercury.

American National Standards Institute (ANSI) Voluntary standards organization for developing national standards.

American Society for Testing and Materials (ASTM) International technical standards organization.

antitrust Federal legislation with the goal of preventing the formation of controlling trusts or monopolies. The intention is to promote competition and regulate trade.

application service provider (ASP) A company that offers software or network application on their servers. Companies subscribe to the service.

assay The analysis of a material or substance to determine its chemical components.

assemble to order The practice in manufacturing of constructing the final product only when an order has been received. This enables manufactures to effectively manage inventory or raw materials and components, and is typical when there are a large number of finished goods that can be built from common materials and components.

assembling The physical act of putting products or product parts together. In manufacturing this often means joining or welding machines, devices, and any other finished product with multiple parts.

assembly line Manufacturing process in which equipment and employees are set up in the order in which the raw materials are used and the final product assembled. Henry Ford is credited with inventing the process, for his automobile manufacturing facility.

ASTM *see* American Society for Testing and Materials.

asynchronous process Two or more process that can run at the same time. Unlike a process like an assembly line that requires one process to be completed before another can begin.

authentication A process to prove identity for access to data or other confidential information.

automated guided vehicle system (AGVS) An inventory management system using vehicles programmed to drive to designated points.

average cost   A way of allocating costs to a unit of a product by using the average of all the costs.

avoirdupois pound   Equivalent to 0.45359237 kilograms.

B2B   *see* business to business.

B2C   *see* business to consumer.

backorder   Generally, an order that was not able to be filled on the date requested. Also refers to the quantity remaining when a manufacturer holds back a certain quantity when the items ship.

balanced scorecard   Method of measuring a company's performance. Developed by Robert Kaplan and David Norton in 1993, it is a method for businesses to determine how well they meet their strategic objectives in areas like return on capital, customer satisfaction, or revenue from new products.

balance of trade   Export minus imports. This represents the net flow of goods between two countries.

bar code   Printed bars on a product or package, such as the UPC code on retail packaging or the ISBN on a book. The bar code represents values like product name and pricing, which can be read and understood when the bar code is scanned.

base demand   The demand for a company's products derived from continuing or existing contracts.

basic producer   A manufacturing company that uses raw materials and natural resources to make items used by other companies to produce finished goods. For example, a steel company producing iron ore or companies that produces glass, rubber, or wood.

batch number   Used for tracking items in inventory or during the production process.

batch picking   Order consolidation method. Requirements from several orders are aggregated to increase efficiency of moving and storing products.

batch processing   In contrast to real-time processing, the execution or programs or processes in sequence, with no interaction among them. In chemical manufacturing, the term applies to processes in which a reactant is added to a reaction vessel and the product is removed after the reaction is carried out.

BEA   *see* U.S. Bureau of Economic Research.

benchmark   A standard used for comparison, or any measurement that is used as a point of comparison for things like performance or productivity.

best practice The optimal method for conducting a business function or manufacturing process.

bill of lading The contract between a shipper or exporter and the transportation company. It limits the liability of the transportation company and acts as the shipper's receipt for the goods and proof that they will be received.

bill of materials (BOM) List of all the materials and components needed to produce a finished item.

bioinformatics In pharmaceutical manufacturing, the use of computers to manage and analyze complex biological data, such as genetic codes.

biological hazard Usually the contamination of food with disease-causing bacteria or other naturally occurring toxin, and a threat to food safety.

biopharmaceuticals Pharmaceutical products made using living organisms that produce or modify the structure and/or function of plants or animals.

biosynthetic In chemical and pharmaceutical manufacturing, making a product with non-natural processes that use biological reactions or enzymes.

biotechnology Use of biological systems or processes for industrial or manufacturing purposes.

BIS *see* Bureau of Industry and Security

blanket order A purchase order that commits a customer to purchasing a specific quantity of an item over specific time. This usually applies to just one item, and includes predetermined delivery dates.

bleed To drain off a gas or liquid, usually slowly, through a valve in order to release pressure.

blind counts In a physical inventory of products, the process of counting the items without knowing the number listed in the inventory record.

blind test The testing of products that are disguised to hide any features that identify them by brand or manufacturer. Evaluating differences between blind tests and branded tests is a way of establishing brand recognition and influence.

BLS *see* U.S. Bureau of Labor Statistics.

book inventory Accounting of inventory by using inventory records, not actually counting the items.

bore The inside diameter of a pipe or tube.

BPI *see* business process improvement.

branded test   The testing of products that are presented with brand or manufacturer information visible. Evaluating differences between blind tests and branded tests is a way of establishing brand recognition and influence.

broker   Intermediary between a shipper and a carrier. *See also* customs broker.

bulk cargo   Goods shipped loose without a mark or item count, such as grain or coal.

bulk commodities   Unprocessed raw materials such as grain, oilseed, or cotton.

Bureau of Industry and Security   Office of the U.S. Department of Commerce that is responsible for implementing and enforcing regulations regarding the export of commercial items.

business to business (B2B)   Sales directly to other business entities, either directly or via a Web site. *See also* wholesaler.

business to consumer (B2C)   Sales directly to consumers, either directly or via a Web site.

business process improvement (BPI)   A method of improving business practices. It involves analyzing activities and eliminating those that do not add value, as well as maintaining or improving productivity, quality, or other business processes that effect performance.

CAD   *see* computer aided design.

CAE   *see* computer aided engineering.

canning   Process of enclosing a food product in a sterilized container, such as a can, jar, or plastic pouch, and heating it until all microorganisms inside the container are killed.

capacity   In manufacturing, this refers to the highest output or production capability. Used to refer to any part of the business or process such as machines, personnel, processes, products, or the entire facility.

capital expenditure (CAPEX)   Financial requirements of an initial investment in a machine, piece of equipment, or facility. For accounting purposes, this cost must be amortized over the life of the machine, equipment, or facility.

cargo   Goods carried in an aircraft, railroad car, ship, barge, or truck.

cargo tonnage   Weight of ocean freight in tons, usually expressed in cubic feet or meters.

carrying cost   The cost associated with having inventory on hand, such as insurance, security, spoilage, and storage.

cartel A group of businesses or nations that act as a single producer to control the market and prices. Cartels are prohibited in the United States.

CAS Chemical Abstracts Service. An organization of the American Chemical Society, they abstract and index chemical literature. CAS numbers identify specific chemicals.

casting Pouring molten materials, typically metal, into a mold and awaiting its hardening or setting.

catch weight In food manufacturing, the actual weight of items whose weight varies by individual item, such as fish or meat. It is used to account for inventory and to set prices.

CCP *see* control point.

cell In a production environment, a group of workstations that work together to produce an item. Also includes the transportation and storage areas associated with the workstations. In shipping, a system used on container vessels to allow containers to be stored vertically.

cellular manufacturing Production process that uses cells to improve productivity, often for production of small lots batches. Teams and cross-training of employees allow for more efficient operations.

centrifugation Manufacturing process in which liquids are spun at high speed, as a way to separate components and cause some particles to settle out of the solution.

certificate of origin (CO) A document that certifies the country of origin for certain goods. Some countries, including the United States, require this certificate for tariff purposes.

certification In food manufacturing, written assurance by an official body that the food item or control system meets requirements. In business in general, written assurance by an official body that an individual meets specified training, testing, or other requirements.

change order Modification of a product order, resulting from revisions in quantity, shipping date, or customer specifications.

chargeback Penalty charged when a shipment does not meet the agreed on terms and conditions.

chemical hazard Danger posed to food in the production process by chemical substances, such as pesticides, detergents, additives, or other toxic materials.

CIM *see* computer integrated manufacturing.

circuit board A panel or card that contains microprocessors, transistors, and other electronic components.

> # Everyone
> ## Knows
> ### Benchmarking Resources
>
> The Association for Manufacturing Excellence (http://www.ame.org) teamed with the American Productivity and Quality Center (APQC) to create a benchmarking community of practice to provide a forum for companies to share best practices.
> APQC (http://www.apqc.org) helps organizations with benchmarking research and reports in areas such as finance, logistics manufacturing, product development, and supply chain.
> The National Association of Manufacturers benchmarking program (http://www.nam.org/benchmarking) provides industry specific data from their Census of Manufacturers.

cleanroom   Room with a highly controlled, sterile environment. Used in manufacturing items like semiconductors and pharmaceuticals.

closed loop recycling   Use of products at the end of their useful life to manufacture the same product.

cloth   Fabric made of mechanically intertwined, interloped, interwoven, or intertangled strands.

CO   *see* certificate of origin.

COGS   *see* cost of goods sold.

combine   Harvesting machine with units for cutting, feeding, threshing, separating, cleaning, collecting, and handling grains or seeds.

commodity   Raw material or primary product that can be bought or sold. Also refers to products like metals, agricultural products, or petroleum that are traded on commodity exchanges.

common carrier   Transportation that is available to anyone in the public. For interstate travel, common carriers must be certified by the Federal Trade Commission.

computer aided design (CAD)   Use of computers to design things like electrical circuits, complex machinery, or other finished products.

computer aided engineering (CAE)   Use of computers to simulate product design and performance.

computer integrated manufacturing (CIM) Use of computers in all plant operations, such as one system for all design, control, and distribution.

concentration The amount of a substance in a stated unit of measure, such as weight per volume.

concurrent engineering Product and process development method that includes simultaneous participation of several functions and teams such as engineering, operations, and accounting. The goal is to shorten the design and development cycle by having events happen at the same time rather than sequentially.

consignee The company or person, usually the buyer, that receives the merchandise or freight shipment. The consignee may also be referred to as the receiver.

consignment inventory Inventory that is in the hands of the customer, but is still owned by the supplier. The customer pays for the inventory only after it is resold or consumed.

consignor The company or person, often the manufacturer, that sends the merchandise or freight shipment. The consignor is also referred to as the shipper.

consortium A group of organizations or companies that share resources and cooperate with each other to reach a common goal.

consultant An outside vendor or supplier who typically offers services. A form of outsourcing.

Consumer Product Safety Commission An independent federal agency responsible for protecting the public by developing and enforcing production and packaging standards.

container In shipping, a box used for transport, primarily ocean shipments. Ocean containers are typically 20 or 40 feet long, 8 or 8.5 feet wide, and 8.5 or 9.5 feet high. They are built to be loaded onto trucks or railroad flat cars for shipment on land.

container load A load of cargo that will fill a container, either by measurement or weight.

containment In pharmaceutical and chemical manufacturing, the process of using materials to keep particles within a specific environment and prevent leakage.

contaminant Foreign matter or impurities that get into food, water, or other preparations and have an adverse impact.

contamination Process by which harmful or unpleasant foreign matter or impurities get into food, water, or other preparations.

continuous flow manufacturing   A production system organized in the order the activities occur, so the product moves efficiently and continuously through the process.

contract carrier   Transportation for one or a small number of shippers under contract. This transportation is not available to the public.

contract manufacturing   Third party that manufactures component or finished parts for another company.

control point   In food processing, the point in the system where inadequate control would result in hazard or contamination. The critical control point (CCP) is the point in the process where factors can be controlled to prevent contamination or hazard.

conveyor   Device that moves freight in a warehouse. Belt conveyors use motors and roller conveyors use gravity.

cooperative   An organization owned by its members, such as agriculture cooperatives that assist farmers in selling their products more efficiently.

cost of good sold (COGS)   The total cost that goes into creating a finished product, including raw materials. In accounting, this is the total value of products sold during a specific time.

country of origin   The country where an item is manufactured or assembled. In apparel manufacturing, this information must appear on the label.

critical control point   *see* control point.

cross dock   A distribution system in which merchandise received is immediately readied for shipment, the items are not put into inventory. This is a way to reduce costs, but requires close synchronization of inbound and outbound shipments.

crude oil   Unrefined liquid petroleum.

customer   The recipient of a product. Customers can be end-users or other manufactures, or someone internal to an organization.

customs   The agency of a government responsible for enforcing import and export fees and regulations.

customs broker   An individual or firm who represents the importer and is licensed to enter and clear imported goods through customs.

cut and sew   Textile manufacturers that specialize in cutting and sewing knitted fabrics.

cycle time   The time it takes for a process to be completed from start to finish.

danger zone Area on or near a machine or piece of equipment where a person may be caught or injured.

deadhead Term for an empty transportation container shipped back to its point of origin.

deadweight tonnage The number of long tons a vessel can transport as cargo, stores, and fuel. It is the difference between the water displacement of the vessel empty or light and that of it full.

demand The product or good customers want. This is usually associated with the consumption of the goods, not for predictions or forecasts.

diamond bit A drill bit with industrial diamonds embedded in the drilling surface.

die Tool used to shape or reshape metal, including tools used to impress a mark in metal.

dilution Adding water or another liquid to weaken the strength of a liquid.

direct cost The cost attributed directly to an item, such as materials and labor involved in producing it.

direct labor Labor costs attributed directly to an item, including wages and benefits, such as production personnel.

discrete manufacturing Manufacturing of distinct items such as a cell phone, a light bulb, a skateboard, a computer, or a dishwasher.

distribution Activities associated with moving goods, such as warehousing, inventory control, shipping, and transportation.

distribution center A warehouse facility that holds a manufacturer's inventory before it is shipped.

distribution resource planning System for understanding inventory demands and how that impacts production processes such as the purchasing of raw materials.

distributor A company that purchases or resells products manufactured by another company.

dock For ocean transport, the cargo area on the shoreline where the vessel ties up. For land transport, the platform for loading and unloading shipments at the facility or terminal.

DOL *see* U.S. Department of Labor.

DOT *see* U.S. Department of Transportation.

downstream The demand side of the supply chain. The wholesale or retail customers who purchase the finished goods.

drop ship The process of shipping a product directly from the supplier to the buyer's customer, without the buyer having to handle the product.

dross Scum on the surface of molten metal, composed of copper, lead oxides, and other elements that float to the top.

dunnage Any materials used to brace or protect cargo, such as wood or paper.

durable goods Manufactured goods designed with an average life span of more than three years, such as appliances or cars.

duty A tax imposed on imported goods by the government, based on the category the product falls into.

dye house In textile manufacturing, this is a business that specializes in preparing and dyeing a fabric to customer specifications.

e-commerce The process of conducting business via computer. Business to consumer e-commerce is the selling of items directly to consumers, usually via a Web site. Business to business e-commerce is the selling of items to other businesses, either as end-users or as component pieces, often via electronic data interchange.

economy of scale The reduction of costs for individual units of a product through production of large quantities.

EDI *see* electronic data interchange

electronic data interchange (EDI) Direct, standardized computer to computer communication between companies.

effluent Wastewater (treated or untreated) that leaves an industrial operation and is often discharged into surface water.

employee An individual who performs work for a company or an individual.

employer A company or individual who hires individuals to perform work.

enterprise A business consisting of one or more establishments under common ownership or control. This may be a single company or a family of companies. Also used as a term to describe a business firm.

enterprise resource planning (ERP) software Computerized system to manage all or most of a manufacturing business. The modular software addresses areas like finances, sales, purchasing, inventory management, and distribution.

EPA *see* U.S. Environmental Protection Agency.

ethernet A local area network connecting computers, printers, workstations, servers, and other computer hardware.

evaporation The process of a liquid changing into a vapor.

export A domestic product sold to foreign resident from a U.S. resident.

extrusion In manufacturing plants that use metal, plastic, or polymers. This is typically a long, uniform item made by forcing the material through a die. In food processing, it is the production of some foods by forcing them through a plate with small holes in it.

fabricator A manufacturer that produces products from raw materials, such as turning steel rods into bolts or turning paper into boxes.

face shield Protective equipment to protect the eyes and the rest of the face. These are usually worn as secondary protection.

facilities The physical plant of a manufacturing company.

FDA *see* U.S. Food and Drug Administration.

Federal Maritime Commission An independent agency that controls ocean going transportation.

Federal Trade Commission Federal agency that enforces consumer protection laws and trade regulations.

fermentation In food and beverage processing, the intentional growth of bacteria, yeast, or mold to cause changes in the food.

fiber In textile manufacturing, a slender and flexible element originating from animals (e.g., wool or rabbit hair), vegetables (e.g., cotton or hemp), minerals (e.g., glass or metal), or synthetic processes. This element is short in length and able to be spun, twisted, or otherwise secured in order to form a strand. In food manufacturing, the part of food fruits, vegetables, and other food items that cannot be digested by humans.

fiber content Percentage of each fiber used in creating the outer fabric of a garment. The U.S. government requires that this information appear on garment labels along with the country of origin.

field warehouse A rented warehouse on the premises of another company.

FIFO *see* first in first out.

fill rate In inventory management, the percentage of orders actually filled in a given period of time.

final assembly The practice of combining components when the actual order is received for the product.

first in first out (FIFO) The practice of rotating inventory and using the oldest products first. It is common in industry sectors in which products have a shelf life. In accounting, this is the method for valuing the cost of goods sold using the cost of the oldest item in inventory.

fixed cost Costs that do not vary with the amount of production. These are costs that must be paid even if production stops, like fixtures, rent, and depreciation on buildings.

FOB *see* free on board.

force majeure In contracts, the clause that exempts the parties, such as the manufacturer or shipper, from fulfilling their contract obligations because of conditions beyond their control like an earthquake or flood.

forecast An estimation of future demand, usually using historic data and adjusted for seasonal fluctuations.

foreign direct investment in the United States Ownership or control of a U.S. business enterprise by a foreign person or entity.

forging Production of a metal item by heat and pressure or hammering.

fractional distillation A process that separates a mixture of several liquids, based on their different boiling points.

free alongside Shipping term defining that the seller must deliver to the goods to the pier, within reach of the vessel's loading equipment. This is the point where the transfer of title or ownership from the seller to the buyer takes place.

free on board (FOB) Shipping term defining that the seller must deliver the goods and load them on a carrier at a specific point. This is the point where the transfer of title or ownership from the seller to the buyer takes place.

free trade agreement Agreement establishing trade between at least two trading partners.

free trade zone Special area of a country without the normal trade barriers such as tariffs and quotas. The goal is to attract business and foreign investment.

freight The goods or materials being transported, or the charges for transportation of goods.

freight forwarder A business that arranges transportation and completes shipping documentation.

friction A resistance to movement between two surfaces, that may produce heat.

FTA *see* free trade agreement.

FTC *see* Federal Trade Commission.

fulfillment Processing customer orders.

fume Airborne particles resulting from the evaporation of solid materials such as metal fumes during welding.

GDP *see* gross domestic product.

general system of preferences (GSP) System enabling developed countries to provide preferential tariff rates to imports from developing countries.

goggles Eye protection that fits directly on the face, and typically used as primary protection or in combination with a face shield or other device.

good manufacturing practices Regulations enforced by the U.S. Food and Drug Administration addressing methods and procedures required for food processing, pharmaceutical manufacturing, medical device, and related manufacturing businesses.

grade Ranking or categorizing items based on features, characteristics, or quality standards. This is a way to address different needs for products with the same functional use.

gross domestic product (GDP) The market value of goods and services produced by labor in the United States, regardless of nationality. In 1991, this became the primary measure of production in the United States, replacing gross national product (GNP).

gross tonnage The volume of the available space on a vessel.

gross weight In shipping, the entire weight of the goods, packaging, and container.

GSP *see* general system of preferences.

hazardous material Substance or material capable of posing a risk to health, safety, and property.

hazardous waste Substance or material produced as a byproduct of a manufacturing or other process and capable of posing a risk to health, safety, and property.

headspace Unfilled area above the food or liquid in a jar.

heat sealing A method of melting adjoining layers of a plastic container to form a seal.

hermetic seal Airtight sealing of a container to prevent air or microorganisms from getting into packaged foods.

Fast
Facts

Material Safety Data Sheets (MSDS)

Manufacturers of chemicals and other substances are required to create labels and material safety data sheets for all such products sold to all customers, both within the industry and members of the general public. There is no specified format, but the Occupational Safety & Health Administration (OSHA) has developed a non-mandatory format (form 174).

Manufacturers and other employers who use chemicals or hazardous substances chemical can search for chemical information from the federal government:

The Occupational Chemical Database (http://www.osha.gov/web/dep/chemicaldata), managed by OSHA and the Environmental Protection Agency, offers identification, properties of, and emergency responses for chemicals by chemical name or CAS number.

The NIOSH databases and other chemical and hazardous materials information (http://www.cdc.gov/NIOSH/topics/chemical-safety) is provided by the U.S. Centers for Disease Control's National Institute for Occupational Safety and Health.

holding company   A corporation that owns enough voting stock in another firm to control management and operations.

hood   Protective device that covers the head and neck and part of the shoulders.

hopper   Funnel or cone shaped device holding dry materials that will later be released through the nozzle at the bottom and mixed with liquid.

horsepower   Measurement of the amount of work done by a machine. It is equivalent to 745.7 watts or 550 foot-pounds per second.

human capital   The capabilities and expertise of individuals in a corporation.

hydration   The addition of water to a substance.

hydraulic   Refers to machines operated or moved by the force of a liquid.

hydrometer An instrument that measures specific gravity of liquids. In food and beverage manufacturing, it is used to measure the concentration of salt, sugar, or alcohol in a product.

hydrostatic pressure The force exerted by a body of fluid at rest, due to the weight of a column of the liquid.

impervious A materials that does not allow another substance to penetrate it.

import A non-domestic product sold to a U.S. resident from a foreign resident.

inbound logistics Transportation and storage of raw materials and others products from suppliers to be put into production or storage.

indirect cost Costs such as overhead or operations costs that cannot be attributed directly to an item.

indirect labor Labor costs not attributable directly to an item, such as management employees.

inland carrier A form of transportation between a port and a point inland.

insourcing Practice of using an in-house department to provide a service.

inspection Testing a product or item to discover errors, standards violations, and other problems.

integrated circuit Circuit with many elements fabricated and interconnected on a single chip of semiconductor material, rather than fabricating and assembling the items separately.

integrated logistics View of the entire supply chain as a single process, and managing them as one entity.

intellectual property Creative works or ideas that can be shared and recreated, emulated, or manufactured by others. Manufacturers protect their intellectual property through patents, trademarks, or trade secrets.

intermodal transportation Moving goods from one location to another via more than one mode of transport, such as using truck and rail or rail and oceangoing vessel.

International Trade Administration Part of the U.S. Department of Commerce, this agency promotes trade and compliance with trade regulations.

interstate commerce The transportation of goods between states.

intrastate commerce The transportation of goods within a state.

invention Any product, machine, design, or way of doing or making things, or any improvement of an existing product, machine, design, or way of doing or making things, that may be patented under the patent laws of the United States.

inventory Number of product units held by a company. May be raw materials, components, or part of a product that is finished or in the process of being made ready for sale.

inventory management The direction and control of activities ensuring that products will be in the right place at the right time.

inventory turns Measurement of how often a company sells or replaces its inventory in a one year period. Higher turnover is good sign, but inventory turn ratios are best used to compare companies within an industry sector because of the differences among sectors.

invoice A bill from the manufacturer requesting payment from the buyer.

irritant A chemical that causes inflammation at the site of contact.

ISO Formerly known as the International Organization for Standards (now named the International Organization for Standardization), this is an international membership organization promoting global standards.

jig A tool that holds parts or component during manufacturing.

just-in-time A process for optimizing manufacturing, it is the practice of having inventory delivered or produced precisely when it is needed for the next process or shipment. The focus is often on the elimination of waste in all areas of the process including things like labor, materials, and space. Sometimes referred to as lean manufacturing.

kaizen Japanese word used to describe a process of continuous improvement in a company. It is a way to eliminate waste, improve quality, and reach higher standards.

key performance indicators (KPI) Measurements of how well a business is meeting its goals. It can be anything a company decides is important to its strategy. In manufacturing, for example, it could be a goal to reuse or recycle a certain percentage of waste from the production process.

knowledge management A way for a company to leverage intellectual property and the wisdom of its employees.

labor productivity Relationship between output and the labor time used to generate the output. This is a measure of how efficiently a manufacturer converts labor into saleable goods. It is expresses as a ratio of output per hour.

landed cost Method of accounting for inventory costs that uses the cost for purchasing materials added to costs such as transportation, import fees, duties, and taxes.

last in first out (LIFO) The practice of using the newest products in inventory first. In accounting, this is the method for valuing the cost of goods sold using the cost of the newest items in inventory.

lead time The time it takes to manufacture a product from the moment it is ordered, including time for processing the purchase order, manufacturing the product, inspection, packaging, and transportation time.

lean manufacturing *see* just-in-time.

letter of credit A document for use in international business transactions. The document is issued by a bank that guarantees payment to the seller when the products are delivered or the sales agreement otherwise fulfilled.

LIFO *see* last in first out.

log A record of data of an activity, job, or process.

logistics management The process of planning, implementing, and controlling the flow of products and materials. It includes functions such as warehousing, inventory management, and order fulfillment.

long ton Unit of weight equal to 2,240 pounds.

machining The physical act of shaping a piece of metal. Machining may be processes such as milling, cutting, turning, boring, drilling, abrading, filing, sawing, or punching.

maintenance In a manufacturing facility, the activities such as cleaning, modifying, or overhauling equipment to maintain proper performance.

manifest The document describing the order being shipped.

manufacturing The act of making a finished good from raw materials.

marginal cost The costs associated with producing one additional unit of output.

mass production Manufacturing products on a large scale, often using assembly line techniques.

mass spectrometer An instrument used to identify materials, using a magnetic field to separate a material's ions and analyze its mass.

master production schedule A process to manage production capacity, especially when demand for a product is expected to exceed manufacturing capacity.

material safety data sheets (MSDS) A document prepared by the manufacturer of chemical products, for those who use the substance in a work setting. It provides information about the properties and hazardous components of the substance, storage and handling considerations, proper disposal of the chemical, and how to treat leaks, spills, fire, and improper human contact.

metric ton A measurement equivalent to 1,000 kilos or 2,204.6 pounds.

mill In the textile industry sector, a company that spins yarn or knits or weaves textiles.

Mine Safety and Health Administration An agency of the U.S. Department of Labor that works to improve the safety and health of mine workers.

monopoly A situation in which a single firm controls competition in a particular market and creates barriers to entry for other firms, allowing them to charge higher prices. Monopolies are prohibited in the United States.

most favored nation A privilege granted by one country to another that allow the advantaged country to pay the lowest duty on products imported to the granting country.

MSDS *see* material safety data sheet.

MSHA *see* Mine Safety and Health Administration.

multinational corporation A company that operates and has direct investment in more than one country.

NAFTA *see* North American Free Trade Agreement.

NAICS *see* North American Industry Classification System.

nanotechnology Creating, manufacturing, and working with objects on the scale of atoms and molecules, roughly defined as being between 0.1 nanometer (about the size of a hydrogen atom) and 100 nanometers (about the size of a virus) in size.

National Fire Protection Association A nonprofit organization focused on fire prevention codes and standards, research, and education.

National Highway Transportation Safety Agency An agency of the U.S. Department of Transportation, this agency focuses on motor vehicle standards and enforcement.

National Institute for Occupational Safety and Health Part of the Centers for Disease Control and Prevention, this agency is responsible for research and recommendations regarding the prevention of work-related injuries and illnesses.

On the Cutting Edge

Nanotechnology Terminology

dendrimer   A polymer with branching parts. Used for targeted drug delivery.

femtotechnology   Materials on the scale of elementary particles such as hadrons and quarks. Smaller than nanotechnology. There are few working applications at this level.

fullerene   Form of carbon bound together and looking a bit like a soccer ball. Fullerenes are also called a buckyballs.

MEMS   Microelectromechanical systems. It refers to microscopic sized machines or systems on silicon.

microfabrication   The process of making miniature structures, such as semiconductors.

microfludics   The study of the behavior and handling of fluids thousands of time smaller than a droplet, where they behave differently than at full scale.

nanobiotechnology   The use of biological or biochemical components in nanotechnology, usually in medical devices.

nanocoatings   Coatings with nanometer sized thickness.

nanocomposites   Plastic compounds with very small particle size used in fillers to improve performance.

National Institute of Standards and Technology   Part of the U.S. Department of Commerce, this non-regulator agency focuses on measurements, standards, and technology.

National Labor Relations Board   An independent federal agency that administers the law governing the relationship between unions and private sector employers.

nationalization   The takeover of a private company by a government.

net tonnage   The cargo capacity of a ship. Like deadweight tonnage, used to determine the carrying capacity of a ship.

net weight   In shipping, the weight of the goods alone, minus that of the packaging, and container.

nanocrystals   Aggregates of atoms with an ordered surface and no interior.

nanofabrication   The building or creating of structures on the nanoscale.

nanometer   A unit of measure equal to one billionth of a meter.

nanooptics   The creating or application of optical structures on the nanoscale.

nanopackaging   Packaging that uses nanomaterials to control properties like vapor permeability, light resistance, and thermal performance, especially for food and beverages.

nanophotonics   The study of the interactions of light at the nanoscale, with applications in industries such as telecommunications and computers.

nanotubes   Hollow carbon structures in the shape of a tube, with structural, electrical, or thermal properties that differ depending on their length, diameter, or other qualities.

nanowires   Tiny wires made of metal or semiconductive materials, for applications in areas like electronics, computers, and medicine.

quantum dots   Semiconductive nanocrystals used in optical or electronic applications.

spintronics   The science of using the spin of electrons rather than their charge to store data.

NFPA   *see* National Fire Protection Association.

NIOSH   *see* National Institute for Occupational Safety and Health.

NIST   *see* National Institute of Standards and Technology.

non-durable goods   Manufactured goods not designed to last more than three years, such as food, cosmetics, or clothing.

North American Free Trade Agreement (NAFTA)   Trade agreement between Canada, Mexico, and the United States, creating the world's largest free trade area.

North American Industry Classification System (NAICS)   The successor of the SIC system, a method of categorizing businesses in Canada, Mexico, and the United States. The system is production oriented and groups industries based on the activity they are primarily engaged in. Most establishment still have both SIC and NAICS codes.

NRC *see* U.S. Nuclear Regulatory Commission.

obsolescence The loss of value or ability to use a product, usually from time or a limitation of the product.

OEM *see* original equipment manufacturer.

Office of the United States Trade Representative Agency of the Executive Office of the President, with the job of negotiating trade agreements, resolving trade disputes, and discussing policy positions.

offshoring A method of outsourcing manufacturing or a business process to a company in another country.

oligopoly A situation in which a small number of firms act together to control a particular market. This allows them to control the supply and charge higher prices.

open loop recycling Process of recycling products at the end of their useful life, and using them to manufacture other products.

order cost The fixed process costs that are incurred each time an item is ordered, such as costs to process the receipt and invoice, and things like machine set up time, inspection time, and time to create the production schedule.

order cycle The time between orders of a specific product.

original equipment manufacturer (OEM) A manufacturer that incorporates the products of another supplier into its own products and markets the products under its own brand.

OSHA *see* U.S. Occupational Safety and Health Administration.

outbound logistics Transportation and storage of finished products from the end of production process to the customer.

outsourcing The use of another company to perform services previously performed on site.

overhead The ongoing expense of operating a business, such as lighting, some administrative personnel, and property taxes or rent.

package A product encased in a cover material such as a box or plastic covering.

pallet A portable platform, often made of wood, that enables a forklift to easily lift, move, and store items.

parent company A company that controls subsidiaries and runs its own business.

pasteurization A heat treatment for food, designed to kill harmful microorganisms. The process involves heating the food

Best
Practice

Shipping goods and materials from a warehouse to the final destination requires a lot of paperwork and coordination, whether you are shipping it domestically or internationally. Here is a sample of the documents commonly used when exporting goods:

- **Shipper's export declaration**–For statistics and preventing exportation of illegal goods.
- **Commercial invoice**–The bill from the buyer to the seller.
- **Certificate of origin**–For certain products or when shipping to some countries.
- **Bill of lading**–The contract between the owner and the carrier.
- **Temporary import certificate**–For merchandise that will be in a foreign company for a limited time only.
- **Insurance certificate**–To cover loss or damage during shipment.
- **Export packing list**–An itemized list of materials, in more detail than a domestic packing list.
- **Import license**–This is the importer's responsibility, but a copy should be included in export documentation.
- **Consular invoice**–Description of goods with information about the value and the parties involved in the shipping. Only required for some countries.
- **Air waybills**–For use with freight shipping by air.
- **Inspection certification**–Documentation by a third party of the specifications of the goods shipped. Required for some goods in some countries.
- **Dock receipt / warehouse receipt**–To transfer accountability when the item moves from a domestic carrier and is left with the ship line for export.
- **Destination control statement**–Part of commercial invoice or ocean or air waybills to notify carrier and others that item can only be exported to certain locations.

item briefly to a temperature below the boiling point. After pasteurization, the final product is usually refrigerated.

patent A right of property granted by the U.S. government to an inventor with the purpose of excluding others from making, selling, or importing the invention in the United States. Patents are issued for a specific period of time.

physical hazard Danger posed to food by an object that gets into the food during production.

plant An establishment or factory. It can also refer to a particular process within an establishment.

post-consumer content Materials that have served their intended uses or reached the end of their useful life, to be used as raw material in the manufacture of a new product.

post-industrial materials Materials generated by manufacturers, such as trimmings or overruns, to be used as raw material in the manufacture of a new product.

preservation In food manufacturing, the process of slowing or stopping food from spoiling, to allow for longer storage time.

preservatives Additives to food or other products that allow for longer storage time.

primary protector Protective device used as the first line of defense. It may be worn alone, but primary protectors are often paired with secondary protective devices.

private carrier Transportation for one firm, that owns or leases the vehicles and does not charge a fee.

private label Products designed and manufactured exclusively for a wholesaler or retailer. Also called a store brand.

procurement The function of obtaining equipment and supplies. In a manufacturing facility, procurement activities include purchasing, inventory control, traffic, and receiving.

product An item manufactured with the purpose of being sold.

productivity See labor productivity.

prototype An initial sample of a product, machine, or other item used to assess the design, utility, and functionality.

purchase order Document showing items and quantities ordered by a buyer.

purification The process of removing contaminants and other impurities from a product or material, by processes such as filtering or sterilization.

quality The state of an item complying with standards and specifications. Often refers to things like appearance, function, or fitness for use.

quality assurance   Activities designed to ensure that processes and products meet standards and specifications.

R&D   *see* research and development.

radio frequency identification (RFID)   A wireless device attached to an object that identifies the object and enables updating of inventory records in real time.

raw material   An unprocessed resource or product used to manufacture a finished item. Examples of raw materials are minerals and crude oil.

reactivity   A substances ability to undergo a chemical change that often results in dangerous side effects like burning or toxic emissions.

real-time processing   In contrast to batch processing, processing of data when it is received, with a fast response that allows for better control of the outcome of the process or activity.

receiving   The activity of accepting delivery of materials or supplies. In a manufacturing facility, this includes an inspection of the material and preparing it for storage or distribution.

refinery   A process or plant that heats crude oil, separating it into its chemical components then distilling them into usable substances.

refractometer   An instrument that measures how light bends and reflects off liquids, to measure soluble solids in things like syrup or jam, or the concentration of salt in water.

remanufacturing   The process of reworking a returned or used product to repair it for resale. Remanufactured items must be labeled as such.

renewable energy   Energy obtained from essentially inexhaustible sources, including wood harvested from wood waste, solar power, wind power, or geothermal power.

replenishment   The process of resupplying inventory, usually from a reserve storage area.

research and development   The process of looking for new solutions, products, or services, using investigation, experimentation, or other systematic or scientific methods.

retailer   Individual or company that sells goods directly to consumers.

request for proposal (RFP)   A document used to request that potential suppliers or vendors prepare and submit a proposal for the needed goods or services.

request for quote (RFQ)   A document used to request that potential suppliers or vendors prepare and submit price quotes for the needed goods or services.

reseller An individual or company that sells items to other businesses or consumers, such as wholesalers and retailers.

reverse logistics The area of logistics that addresses the movement of products after sale and delivery to the customer, such as product returns.

RFID *see* radio frequency identification.

RFP *see* request for proposal.

RFQ *see* request for quote.

risk management The process of reviewing and understanding the dangers in a process or activity and setting up processes and policies to reduce the risk. In manufacturing, risk management includes activities like implementing safety and control measures, as well as identifying and managing regulatory requirements.

safety The condition of being protected from activities, events, or processes that can cause death, injury, illness, or damage.

sample Small quantities of a fluid or material used for analysis or testing.

seasonality Variability in the demand for a product or material over a specific time interval, such as year to year. This is used to explain the differences in demand for items used in different seasons such as ski equipment or other recreational products.

secondary protector Protective equipment that is worn in combination with a primary protective device.

self-assembly The ability of living cells to assemble themselves into an orderly structure. In nanotechnology, this may even include inanimate materials.

semiconductor An element with electrical conductivity between insulator and conductors, and commonly changed by light, heat, electric, or magnetic fields. Silicon (Si) and germanium (Ge) are single element semiconductors.

sequestrants A compound used to hold metals or other materials to prevent them from coming out of solution, and to render them inactive.

service level agreement (SLA) A contract that enumerates the services that will be provided to the customer. This usually addresses areas such as availability of the service, customer support activities, and security issues.

shaping The act of altering the form, configuration, or contour of a part or component and can include the removal of material.

shared services The process of consolidating resources to run like a separate business unit, to save costs and provide services to the parent company and sometimes to customers or other external entities.

shelf life The amount of time before a product becomes unstable. This is an important measurement in food and pharmaceutical manufacturing.

shipper The individual or company that needs good transported.

shipping lane In general, the logical route between the original shipment location and the delivery location. In ocean shipping, the routes that commercial vessels typically follow between ports.

shipping manifest Document that lists the items, weight, and destination names and addresses for a particular shipment, whether the entire load is destined for one location or many.

short ton Unit of weight equal to 2,000 pounds.

SIC codes *see* Standard Industrial Classification

Six Sigma A system of measuring quality and control in a manufacturing facility, to reduce the error rate to less than 3.4 defects in one million, or within six standard deviations (six sigma) of normal. The term originated at Motorola.

SKU *see* stock keeping units.

SLA *see* service level agreement.

slurry A liquid containing a high suspension of solids, used to facilitate movement of the liquid through pipes.

solar power Energy generated from the heat or light of the sun.

solid state The electronic properties of a crystalline material, as opposed to vacuum and gas-filled tubes that transmit electricity.

SOP See standard operating procedure

sourcing The process of identifying suppliers or vendors for materials or services needed by a manufacturer.

specification Document prepared by manufacturers that describes requirements, design, behavior, or other characteristics of a material, component, or system.

stabilizer In food manufacturing, a substance that allows certain items to remain in a homogeneous state. In chemical manufacturing, a substance that inhibits reaction between two or more chemicals.

standard cost In inventory costing, the material, labor, and machine costs used to calculate cost of the finished item.

Standard Industrial Classification (SIC) Originally developed in the 1930s, this system is used in the United States to group establishments into industries, and is a manufacturing oriented system. In 1997, it was replaced with the North American Industry Classification System. Most establishment still have both SIC and NAICS codes.

standard operating procedure (SOP) Written procedures that describe the steps and processes in normal operations, and are used to control production and quality.

stock keeping units (SKU) Numbers and bar codes used to define the specific style, and color of an item, used for planning, budgeting, tracking, and retailing purposes.

store brand *see* private label.

subsidiary A wholly or partially owned company that is part of a large corporation. Foreign subsidiaries are incorporated separately under the laws of the country where they are located.

supplier Any company or individual that provides goods or services to a company.

supply chain The sequence of processes and activities involved in the manufacture and distribution of products, from raw materials to the finished good in the hand of the customer.

supply chain management The process of planning and administering all the activities and process involved in the manufacture and distribution of products, including collaborating with suppliers, vendors, and other third parties. Ideally, this integration extends beyond the individual manufacturer to manage the process across all the companies in the process.

Surface Transportation Board An agency of the U.S. Department of Transportation the regulates railroads and trucking.

surfactant A substance with cleansing properties.

tare weight The allowance made for the weight of an empty container and packaging materials, in order to determine the net weight of the items.

tariff A tax assessed by a government on imported and exported goods.

task rotation Switching employees between tasks to allow rest and prevent trauma.

technology transfer The process of sharing discoveries and knowledge gained in research and development in government or educational laboratories to the commercial sector.

textile   A flexible fabric.

thermal processing   Processes that use heat such as canning or bottling in the food industry.

thermophysical properties   The properties that affect how a material can be heated, such as the ability of the material to conduct or store heat.

third party logistics   Outsourcing services like warehousing and distribution to a service provider.

throughput   A way to measure the output of a warehouse, using the total units received and total shipped.

TIFA   *see* Trade And Investment Framework Agreement.

time to market   The amount of time between the beginning of the research and feasibility assessment stage and the delivery of the first production unit.

torque   A turning force applied to a mechanism or shaft to cause it to rotate.

total quality management (TQM)   A system of controlling and measuring quality processes and policies, from product development to sales and service. The focus is on build into the product the qualities that are important to the customer.

toxic   A poisonous substance, capable of having a harmful effect.

Trade And Investment Framework Agreement   An agreement that provides a framework for future trade relationships.

trade deficit   The amount by which the value of imports exceeds the value of exports.

trade secret   Confidential information about a product or process that a manufacturer or company keeps secret to have advantage over the competition.

trademark   Protected words, names, symbols, sounds, or colors used by a manufacturer to distinguish a product from those made by other companies. Unlike a patent, a trademark can be renewed forever, as long as it is still in use in commerce.

transistor   An electronic device that amplifies electronic signals, and made from semiconductive material.

turbine   A machine for converting mechanical energy into rotary power using the energy of steam or a fluid.

ultrasonic   A vibrating wave above the upper frequency limit of the human ear, generally above 16 kilocycles per second.

union   An association of workers organized together to maintain or improve working conditions, wages, and employee benefits.

unit cost The costs associated with making a single unit of a product.

universal product code (UPC) A standard product numbering systems used in the retail industry. The code identifies the manufacturer and the product name.

upstream The supply side of the supply chain. The vendors, suppliers, and manufacturers who provide raw materials and other goods and services that enable the manufacture to produce a product.

U.S. Bureau of Economic Research An agency of the U.S. Department of Commerce, this bureau provides timely information about the U.S. economy.

U.S. Bureau of Labor Statistics An independent government agency with the mission of collecting, analyzing, and disseminating business.

U.S. Chemical Safety Board An independent government agency with the mission of investigating chemical accidents and making recommendations for the industry.

USDA *see* U.S. Department of Agriculture.

U.S. Department of Agriculture Federal agency providing information and guidance for food, agriculture, and natural resource providers and manufacturers.

U.S. Department of Labor Government agency that promotes the welfare of job seekers, wage earners, and retirees by improving working conditions, advocating for workers and employers, and administering federal laws in the area of employment.

U.S. Department of Transportation Federal agency that focuses on the transportation system and keeping travelers and goods safe.

U.S. Environmental Protection Agency Government agency responsible for environmental science, research, education, and assessment.

U.S. Food and Drug Administration Part of the U.S. Department of Health and Human Services, this agency protects the public health by regulating standards and labeling of food, drugs, and related products.

U.S. Nuclear Regulatory Commission An independent federal agency with the goal of ensuring that businesses and individuals safely use nuclear power and radioactive materials in all applications.

U.S. Occupational Safety and Health Administration   A department of the U.S. Department of Labor, that provides education, research, information, and enforcement in the area of workplace health and safety.

U.S. Patent and Trademark Office   An agency of the U.S. Department of Commerce, this office registers trademarks, issues patents, and disseminates patent and trademark information as a way to protect businesses, individuals, and consumers.

vacuum packed   A food packaging method using an air-tight package and removal of all air prior to sealing as a way to prevent the growth of microorganisms.

validation   A process of establishing evidence that a design, product, or process will perform consistently and to specifications.

valve   A device used to control the rate of flow of a fluid or gas, and used an automatic or manual safety device.

variable cost   Costs that fluctuate depending on the number of items produced by an activity. If the production activity stops, the variable cost is zero.

vendor   The manufacturer or distributor of a product or material.

viscosity   A measurement of the consistency of a fluid.

wafer   In semiconductor manufacturing, a thin slice sawed from a cylindrical ingot of pure, crystalline silicon.

wafer fabrication   The operations that put a circuit or device on a silicon wafer.

warehouse   A storage place for products, as well as where they are received and shipped.

wholesaler   An individual or business that purchases and resells the products of another manufacturer.

workflow   A system of activities that represent a business process, such as the manufacture of a product from accumulation of raw materials to the completion of the finished product.

workstation   An area and set of machines and equipment used to do a specific set of tasks.

World Trade Organization   International organization dealing with trade issues among member nations.

Chapter 6

Resources

Associations and Organizations

There are a large number of industry and trade associations in each of the manufacturing sectors, in addition to some industry-wide organizations. Below is a list of some of the organizations that look at the industry as a whole or a specific aspect of it. To see a list of all the associations in any industry or sector, visit your local library or career center to use the printed or online version of *The Encyclopedia of Associations*. There are two editions—U.S. and international.

General or Cross-Sector

American Association of Engineering Societies   An umbrella organization that works with member societies to advance the knowledge and practice of engineering. (http://www.aaes.org)

American Society for Quality   A professional association that advances the concepts of quality and improvement, and administers the Malcolm Baldrige National Quality Award. (http://www.asq.org)

American Society of Safety Engineers   Professional organization for health, safety, and environment professionals. Provides advocacy, education, and a job search function. (http://www.asse.org)

American Society of Transportation and Logistics   Professional organization for professionals in the fields of logistics, supply chain, and transportation. Provides networking, certification, and other resources. (http://www.astl.org)

American Welding Society   Trade organization for those in the welding and related joining technologies. Provides education, certification, are career guidance. (http://www.aws.org)

Association for Operations Management   Organization focused on operations management, inventory, supply chain, and logistics. Provides advocacy for the industry, education and training, and certification. (http://www.apics.org)

Association of Manufacturing Excellence   Association dedicated to helping manufacturers with continuous improvement, through techniques such as lean tools, kaizen, and lean accounting. (http://www.ame.org)

ASTM   Formerly known as the American Society for Testing and Materials, this is a standards development organization that focuses on technical standards for materials, products, and systems. Provide training, testing, directories of equipment manufacturers, testing laboratories, and consultants and expert witnesses. (http://www.astm.org)

Council of Supply Chain Management Professionals   Organization for supply chain management personnel. Provides education, research, and a career center. (http://www.cscmp.org)

Institute for Supply Management   Professional organization for supply management professionals. Provides standards, certification, education, and research. (http://www.ism.ws)

IEEE   Formerly known as the Institute of Electrical and Electronics Engineers, this is a technical organization for engineers and manufacturers in industry sectors such as aerospace, biomedical engineering, computers, and electronics. Provide standards, education, councils and technical communities, and other resources. (http://www.ieee.org)

Institute for Molecular Manufacturing   Organization that funds and conducts research into nanotechnology. They advocate for the industry, provides research and industry information, and sponsors projects in many applications of nanotechnology. (http://www.imm.org)

Institute of Industrial Engineers   Professional society for industrial engineers and professionals involved in quality and productivity issues. Provides training, research, and technical resources. (http://www.iienet.org)

Manufacturers Alliance   Industry organization for senior executives in all manufacturing sectors. Focuses on economic research, problem solving, and networking for senior executives in manufacturing. (http://www.mapi.net)

Minerals, Metals and Materials Society   Professional organization for the entire range of materials and engineering—from minerals processing and processing of primary metals to the advanced application of materials. Provides education and training, certification, and industry information. (http://www.tms.org)

National Association for Manufacturing Sciences   Research consortium of North American corporations, with a focus on collaboration and translating research into real-world applications. (http://www.ncms.org)

National Association of Manufacturers   Trade association for executives and professionals in the manufacturing industry. Shares information with the public about manufacturing, focuses on policies and regulatory matters, and advocates for educational opportunities. (http://www.nam.org)

National Council for Advanced Manufacturing   Trade association for companies, organizations, and individuals who share their goal: To strengthen the U.S. manufacturing industry and enhance the competitiveness of U.S. manufactures in the global community. (http://www.nacfam.org)

National Tooling and Machining Association   Trade organization for professionals in the custom precision manufacturing industry, who provide machine tools and related equipment to nearly every other manufacturing sector. Provides education, advocacy, and industry information. (http://www.ntma.org)

Remanufacturing Institute   An industry organization for remanufacturing and related businesses. Provides industry research and policy advocacy as well as other resources. (http://www.reman.org)

Society for Maintenance and Reliability Professionals   Professional organization for maintenance professionals in manufacturing and others industries. Provides education, certification, and other resources. (http://www.smrp.org)

Supply-Chain Council   International organization for companies in many industries including manufacturing and distribution. Provides benchmarking information, education, and career development. (http://www.supply-chain.org)

Tooling, Manufacturing, and Technologies Association   For professionals in metalworking, manufacturing, and technology industries. Provides advocacy and industry information. (http://www.themta.org)

Warehousing Education and Research Council   Professional organization for warehouse management professionals. Provides education, research, and benchmarking metrics. (http://www.werc.org)

Sector Specific

Aerospace Industries Association   Professional organization for manufacturers and suppliers in civilian and military aircraft, space systems, aircraft engines, missiles, and related fields. Provides industry information and standards, as well as a job search feature. (http://www.aia-aerospace.org)

American Composites Manufacturers Association   Trade organization for composite manufacturers and supplies. Provides education, technical resources, and policy advocacy. (http://www.acmanet.org)

American Foundrymen's Society   Professional organization for the diecasting and metalcasting industry sector. Provides advocacy, education, and a career center. (http://www.afsinc.org)

American Iron and Steel Institute   Trade organizations for manufacturers, suppliers, and others in the steel industry. Provides industry information and advocates for the industry. (http://www.steel.org)

American Society of Agricultural and Biological Engineers   Professional organization for engineers and others involved in engineering in the fields of agriculture, food, and biological systems. Provides technical information, education, and standards (http://www.asabe.org)

Association for Manufacturing Technology   Trade organization for companies in the machinery and equipment manufacturing industry sector, including those involved in areas such as design, automation, assembly, and inspection and testing. Provides industry standards, market and business development information, advocacy, and research support. (http://www.amtonline.org)

Biomedical Engineering Society   Professional organization for biomedical engineers and bioengineers. Provides education, accreditation of educational programs, and a career center. (http://www.bmes.org)

Biotechnology Industry Organization Professional association for organizations in the biotechnology arena, such as healthcare, agriculture, industrial biotechnology, and the environment. Provides advocacy and business development. (http://www.bio.org)

National Association for Surface Finishing Trade association for professionals in the surface finishing, electroplating, and metal finishing industry sector. Provide advocacy and industry information. (http://www.nasf.org)

Society for Mining, Metallurgy, and Exploration Professional organization for individuals in the mining and mineral community. Provides education, industry information, and a career center. (http://www.smenet.org)

Society of Petroleum Engineers Organization for professionals in the petroleum industry. Provides industry information and research, publications, and a career center. (http://www.spe.org)

Unions

Labor unions act as an advocates for their members, as well as providing education, working to improve wages and benefits, helping members find employment, and promoting safety and health for the workforce and within the workplace. Most unions represent workers who do a particular type of work, within any manufacturing industry sector. Union members pay dues and are run by leaders nominated and elected by the membership. Not all manufacturing plants are unionized, and in those that are, not all employees are necessarily union members or represented by a union.

Strikes are what a lot of people think of when they hear the word union. But they are a last resort to deal with a labor issue and must be voted on by union members. Most contract negotiations and agreements between labor and management are reached with bargaining and mediation, and no work interruption.

AFL-CIO The American Federation of Labor and Congress of Industrial Organizations is a federation of 56 national and international labor unions, representing more than 11 million workers. (http://www.aflcio.org)

Bakery, Confectionery, Tobacco Workers and Grain Millers International Union Represents workers in Canada and the

United States. Affiliated with the AFL-CIO and Canadian Labour Congress. (http://www.bctgm.org)

Glass, Molders, Pottery, Plastics and Allied Workers International Union   Represents more than 40,000 workers in the United States. Affiliated with the AFL-CIO. (http://www.gmpiu.org)

International Association of Machinists and Aerospace Workers   Represents workers in Canada and the United States. Affiliated with the AFL-CIO. (http://www.goiam.org)

International Brotherhood of Boilermakers, Iron Ship Builders, Blacksmiths, Forgers and Helpers   Represents more than 100,000 workers in Canada and the United States. (http://www.boilermakers.org)

International Brotherhood of Electrical Workers   Represents more than 725,000 workers in the Canada and the United States. Affiliated with the AFL-CIO. (http://www.ibew.org)

International Brotherhood of Teamsters   Represents more than 1.4 million workers in Canada, Puerto Rico, and the United States. (http://www.teamster.org)

International Chemical Workers Union   Represents workers in the United States. Part of the United Food and Commercial Workers Union. (http://www.icwuc.org)

Sheet Metal Workers International Association   Represents more than 150,000 workers in the Canada, Puerto Rico, and the United States. Affiliated with the AFL-CIO and the Canadian Labour Congress. (http://www.smwia.org)

United Automobile, Aerospace, and Agricultural Implement Workers of America   Represents more than 513,000 workers in Canada, Puerto Rico, and the United States. This union is also called the United Auto Workers union. Affiliated with the AFL-CIO. (http://www.uaw.org)

United Food and Commercial Workers International Union   Representing more than 1.3 million members in Canada and the United States. (http://www.ufcw.org)

United Mine Workers   Represents workers in Canada and the United States. (http://www.umwa.org)

United Steelworkers Union   Recently merged with the Paper, Allied-Industrial, Chemical, and Energy (PACE) Workers International Union Represents more than 850,000 workers in Canada and the United States. Affiliated with the AFL-CIO. (http://www.usw.org)

Certifications

Certification is a way to demonstrate knowledge and competency in a particular skill. There are many organizations that offer certification and training. CareerVoyages.gov and Career One Stop both offer a list of certifications by industry and job title; and many industry organizations have a discussion of relevant certifications. Below is a sample of certification organizations.

American Society for Quality   A membership organization focusing on quality and improving organizational processes. Offers training and certifications in manufacturing including: calibration technician, pharmaceutical GMP professional, quality auditor, quality engineer, and software quality engineer. (http://www.asq.org)

American Welding Society   A membership organization that focuses on the science, technology, and application of welding and related joining disciplines. Offers training and certification in welding including: welding inspector, radiographic interpreter, welding sales representative, welding engineer, and welder. (http://www.aws.org)

Association for Operations Management   Membership organization that focuses on operations management—production, inventory, purchasing, logistics, and the like. Offers training, and certification in production and inventory management and supply chain. (http://www.apics.org)

Association for the Advancement of Medical Instrumentation   Industry organization focused on medical instrumentation and technology. Certifications include: biomedical equipment technician and laboratory equipment specialist. (http://www.aami.org)

ETA International   The Electronics Technician Association focuses on programs, education, and certification for professionals in electronics-related professions in fields like fiber optics, biomedical, aviation, and industrial electronics. Certifications include: aerospace fiber optics fabricator, biomedical equipment technician, and radio frequency identification technical specialist. (http://www.eta-i.org)

Institute of Hazardous Materials Management   Certification organization that focuses on health and safety and the general management of hazardous materials and related areas.

Professional Ethics

Maria and Gerry work for a non-unionized manufacturer. Gerry thinks the plant should be unionized but Maria disagrees. The company executives and managers have so far been quiet about the issue, but they know what is going on. Gerry is avidly supporting passage of the Employee Free Choice Act that is on Congress' docket, and he is pressuring Maria to support the cause.

Maria does not have strong feelings about starting a union and wants to sit on the sidelines. She knows that this pending legislation is designed to strengthen protections for employees seeking to form a union, including enabling the National Labor Relations Board to certify a union of the majority of employees in the workplace sign-up. She's uncomfortable with political issues like this, but is afraid to hurt Gerry's feelings if she does not support his cause.

Should Maria support a cause she does not believe in strongly, just because her good friend does? Is it okay for her to sit on the sidelines and let others decide an important workplace issue?

After thinking about this for a while, Maria decided to tell Gerry that she would not get involved. She let him know that she would support him and his hard work on the issue, but that she had ambivalent feelings about unions and political issues. At first Gerry was upset, but he understood. His goal was not to force people to unionize, but to organize and encourage those employees who did want to work toward that goal.

Certifications include: hazardous materials manager, hazardous materials manager-in-training, and hazardous materials practitioner. (http://www.ihmm.org)

Institute for Supply Management   Organization that focuses on research and education of supply management professionals across industries. Certifications include: professional in supply management and purchasing manager. (http://www.ism.ws)

NACE International Organization dedicated to corrosion engineering and corrosion control. Offers training and certification. Certifications include: corrosion technologist, protective coating specialist, and chemical treatment specialist. (http://www.nace.org)

National Institute for Certification in Engineering Technologies Organization that certifies individuals in engineering technologies and related disciplines. Certifications include those for fire alarm system technicians, geotechnical engineering technicians, and industrial instrumentation technicians. (http://www.nicet.org)

National Registry of Environmental Professionals Organization providing training and certification for environmental engineers, technologists and technicians, managers, and scientists. Certifications include: associate environmental professional, hazardous and chemical materials manager, indoor air quality manager, and mold inspector. (http://www.nrep.org)

Retail Bakers of America Organization focusing on retail bakers, suppliers, and others in the industry. Offers education and industry information, as well as certifications such as: baker and journey baker. (http://www.rbanet.com)

Society for Protective Coatings Membership organization offering standards, education, and certification for professionals in the protective coating industry. Certifications include protective coating specialist. (http://www.sspc.org)

Society of Manufacturing Engineers Organization promoting manufacturing and careers in the industry. Certifications include: engineering manager, manufacturing engineer, and manufacturing technologist. (http://www.sme.org)

Society of Tribologists and Lubrication Engineers Organization for professionals in lubrication engineering. Offers education and certification in lubrication, metalworking fluids, and oil monitoring. (http://www.stle.org)

Books and Periodicals

Books

Big Cotton. By Stephen Yafa (Viking, 2005). Looks at the beginnings of the industry and includes discussion of Eli Whitney, Samuel Slater, and other important industry figures.

Boeing versus Airbus: The Inside Story of the Greatest International Competition in Business. By John Newhouse (Random House, 2008). A look at the two aviation giants, how they got that way and how they influence the industry today.

Chrysler: The Life and Times of an Automotive Genius. By Vincent Curcio (Oxford University Press, 2000). The story of Walter Chrysler and his rise to become an industrial giant.

The Deal Maker: How William C. Durant made General Motors. By Axel Madsen (Wiley, 1999). The story of the formation of General Motors and Mr. Durant's innovative spirit.

History of Manufactures in the United States. By Victor S. Clark (McGraw-Hill, 1916). Two volume set looking at all aspects of the industry from 1607 to 1860 including discussion of ships, railroads, iron and steel, textiles and cotton, and industrial life.

The Maverick and His Machine: Thomas Watson Sr. and the Making of IBM. By Kevin Maney (Wiley, 2004). The story of how he transformed a small machine company into a worldwide company, and turned information into big business.

Meet You in Hell: Andrew Carnegie, Henry Clay Frick, and the Bitter Partnership that Transformed America. By Les Standiford (Crown, 2005). The back story of the rise of the steel manufacturing business, the rivalry between these industrial giants, and the dangers of big business.

The People's Tycoon: Henry Ford and the American Century. By Steven Watts (Vintage, 2005). About the automobile pioneer and his impact on American industry.

Robert Wood Johnson: The Gentleman Rebel. By Lawrence G. Foster (Lillian Press, 1999). The story of the founder of Johnson & Johnson and his achievements and philanthropic efforts.

Periodicals

There are a tremendous number of magazines in every sector of the manufacturing industry. Journals and magazines cover the industry as a whole, some address specific topics like logistics, and sector-specific publications address narrow topics. Many magazines, newsletters, and journals are published by industry associations and available as a benefit of membership. Others are subscription based. Below is a sampling of some publications.

To find other magazines of interest, you can do a general search online. Or you can visit your local library and use the printed or online versions of the two classic serials directories. *The Standard Periodical Directory* is a single volume listing more than 60,000 journals, magazines, newsletters, and newspapers. *Ulrich's Periodicals*

Directory is a multivolume set listing more than 225,000 international journals, magazines, and newsletters.

Baking & Snack Monthly. For managers and decision makers in development, production, and distribution of grain-based foods. (http://www.bakingbusiness.com)

Beverage Industry Monthly. For managers, operations staff, research, and sales and marketing professionals in production, distribution, or retailing in the beverage industry. (http://www.bevindustry.com)

Candy Industry Monthly. For managers, operations staff, research, and sales and marketing professionals in production, distribution, repackaging, and retailing in the confectionery industry. (http://www.candyindustry.com)

Chemical Week Weekly. Technical and business information for professionals in chemical, petrochemical, specialty chemicals, and related industries. (http://www.chemweek.com)

Cleanrooms Monthly. For contamination control professionals in industries that require a clean manufacturing environment such as semiconductor, biopharmaceutical, electronics, and food processing. (http://www.cleanrooms.com)

Conformity Monthly. Regulatory and design information for electrical engineering professionals. (http://www.conformity.com)

Food Engineering Monthly. For management, operations and production, and professionals in the food and beverage industries. (http://www.foodengineeringmag.com)

Hydrocarbon Processing Monthly. For engineers, designers, operations personnel, and others in refineries, petrochemical plants, and gas processing facilities. (http://www.hydrocarbonprocessing.com)

Inbound Logistics Monthly. For business logistics managers and other inventory and logistics professionals. (http://www.inboundlogistics.com)

Industry Week Weekly. For executives, operations professionals, engineers, and others in all sectors of manufacturing. (http://www.industryweek.com)

Ink World Magazine 10 issues a year. For professionals in development, manufacture, and distribution of inks, coatings, and allied products. (http://www.inkworldmagazine.com)

Logistics Management Monthly. For executives, managers, and other professionals in logistics and supply chain management. (http://www.logisticsmgmt.com)

Meat and Poultry   Monthly. For professionals in meat and poultry processing. (http://www.meatpoultry.com)

Metal Bulletin   Weekly. For professionals in ferrous and non-ferrous metal manufacturing and distribution. (http://www.metalbulletin.com)

Material Handling Management   Monthly. For inventory, materials, and distribution managers and executives in manufacturing. (http://www.mhmonline.com)

Modern Plastics   Monthly. For management, engineering, sales and marketing, and other professionals in horizontal plastics processing and allied fields. (http://www.modplas.com)

Perfumer & Flavorist   Monthly. For management, buyers, sales and marketing, and other professionals in the flavor and fragrance industry. (http://www.perfumerflavorist.com)

Quality Digest   Monthly. For management and other professionals interested in quality, including standards, inspection, and testing. (http://www.qualitydigest.com)

Wine Business Magazine   Monthly. For management and other professionals in winemaking and grape growing. (http://www.winebusiness.com)

Everyone Knows

Certified Versus Licensed

Licenses are issued by governmental agencies, often the state, and are required by law to work or practice a particular occupation in many industries. To become licensed, a candidate typically has to have formal education or some form of training, experience, and successful completion of an examination. In some cases, there are also residency or citizenship requirements.

Certification is a voluntary process offered by industry organizations and is not mandated by law. However, some licenses require certification as a step in the licensure process.

Manufacturing occupations that typically require a license: accountant, electrician, engineer, environmental health scientist, geologist, and pharmacist.

Web Sites

General Information

Best Manufacturing Practices Center of Excellence   Something of a clearinghouse for various tips and strategies related to all areas of manufacturing, this site surveys different companies and shares their best practices with others in the industry. (http://www.bmpcoe.org)

Manufacturing.gov   This site describes itself as being "dedicated to providing the most comprehensive and current information on issues surrounding the competitiveness of American manufacturers and service industries." It tracks government initiatives and provides in-depth analysis of various manufacturing policy reports. (http://www.manufacturing.gov)

Manufacturing.net   This Web site is a good place to read about the latest trends and developments in various manufacturing fields. A number of executives visit and post to this site, which makes it one of the more dependable manufacturing news sources on the Web. (http://www.manufacturing.net)

Education and Training

General Apprenticeships

Apprenticeships are offered by individual companies, unions, or other organizations. This is usually in conjunction with the U.S. Department of Labor Office of Apprenticeship, which sets program standards including how apprentice are paid, the amount of supervision, and measurement of the apprentice's progress. There are literally hundreds of occupations that can be learned via apprenticeships. Here is a sample of some manufacturing apprenticeships available in May 2009: Bakery-machine mechanic, CNC setup programmer, die designer, electrician, fastener technologist, machinist, plastic process technician, quality control technician.

Check with your employer, union, or industry organization to find out about apprenticeships. The following resources provide links to local and industry-specific programs.

Career Voyages   Government site run by the U.S. Department of Labor and the U.S. Department of Education. Includes information about apprenticeships in advanced manufacturing, aerospace, biotechnology, and information technology. (http://www.careervoyages.gov)

U.S. Department of Labor Employment and Training Division Office of Apprenticeship This site provides links to national, regional, and state apprenticeship agencies. These agencies can provide job seekers and employees with information about program sponsors and appropriate local programs. (http://www.doleta.gov/oa)

Sector-specific Apprenticeships

Boilermakers National Apprenticeship Program Apprenticeship program offered by the International Brotherhood of Boilermakers, Iron Ship Builders, Blacksmiths, Forgers and Helpers. (http://www.bnap.com)

International Union of Operating Engineers Offers training and apprenticeship programs for jobs such as heavy equipment operator or stationary engineer. (http://www.iuoe.org)

National Institute for Metalworking Skills Apprenticeship program for occupations such as: machinist, toolmaker, and CNC setup programmer. The program was developed with the U.S. Department of Labor and several manufacturing industry organizations. (http://www.nims-skills.org)

Colleges and Universities

Many universities, two- and four-year colleges, and vocational schools have engineering or manufacturing related programs and majors such as industrial safety, nanotechnology, robotics, or welding. Schools also offer sector specific programs and degrees in areas like agribusiness, biotechnology, chemistry, computer science, environmental sciences, food sciences, and mining. There are many different ways to search for an educational program and school. The career and college section of your local public library or bookstore will have college directories and other helpful resources. Below are a few resources to get you started.

When you are reviewing colleges or vocational programs, including online schools, look for schools that are accredited by accrediting agencies recognized by the U.S. Secretary of Education. Students who study at these accredited institutions are eligible for federal benefits such as financial aid. In addition, some employers, institutions, or licensing boards will only recognize a degree from an institution accredited by an agency recognized by the Department of Education. To find out if a school is accredited, visit the Department of Education Office of Postsecondary Education and search their database of accredited institutions and programs: http://ope.ed.gov/accreditation.

When you are considering programs and schools, there are some other things to consider. If you plan to study a specific occupation or industry-related program, look for schools that work with recognized industry groups and use industry standards when designing their curriculum. Also, ask to see records of graduates who found work in the field.

If the school is unknown to you, it is important to ensure the legitimacy of the school, program, or credential offered. There are companies that offer degrees or certificates for little or no work and essentially sell worthless degrees or credentials to unsuspecting individuals. Avoid schools that:

➡ Offer you a degree for just having life or work experience. Although they may allow a few credits for specific work experience, accredited schools will never allow you to substitute experience for doing the work.

➡ Let you get your degree without ever attending a class. Legitimate schools and online programs always require attendance and coursework.

➡ Accept payment on a per-degree basis. Accredited schools charge by the number of credits or courses you take, or by the semester or term. They never charge a flat fee for a degree.

➡ Advertise via spam or pop-up advertisements. Legitimate programs never advertise that way.

America's Best Colleges　Print directory published annually by *U.S. News & World Report*.

Barron's　Publisher with college guides and resources, including annual directories such as *Barron's Compact Guide to Colleges* and *Barron's Profiles of American Colleges Northeast*. (http://www.barronseduc.com)

Career One Stop　A site sponsored by the U.S. Department of Labor, with career resources and an education search function. Individuals can search for a school by occupation name or keywords, as well as by location and education level. (http://www.careerinfonet.org)

Career Voyages Career site run by the U.S. Department of Education and the U.S. Department of Labor. Students can search for community colleges and four-year colleges by industry and location. (http://www.careervoyages.gov)

College Board Organization that provides testing and college planning services for students. It offers a college matchmaker service, allowing students to search for schools by program of study, as well as other criteria like location, costs, and type of school, including two- or four-year programs. (http://www.collegeboard.com)

College Navigator Operated by the U.S. Department of Education. Students can search by name of school, location, major, and other criteria like cost, campus setting, and enrollment. Includes

Fast Facts

Several publishers specialize in publishing trade magazines.

BNP Media publishes more than 40 publications, including: *Assembly, Adhesives & Sealants Industry, Ceramic Industry, Food Engineering, Industrial Heating, Industrial Safety & Hygiene News, Packaging Strategies, Pollution Engineering, Prepared Foods, Quality*, and *World Trade*. (http://www.bnpmedia.com)

Cygnus Business Media publishes more than 40 magazines, including: *Fabricating & Metalworking, Feed & Grain, Food Logistics, Industrial Machinery Digest*, and *Supply & Demand Chain Executive*. (http://www.cygnusb2b.com)

Penton Media publishes more than 100 magazines, including: *American Machinist, Beef, Bulk Transporter, Forging, Foundry Management & Technology, Industry Week, Machine Design, Material Handling, Medical Design, Microwaves & RF, Outsourced Logistics, Refrigerated Transporter*, and *Welding Magazine*. (http://www.penton.com)

Reed Business Information publishes more than 80 magazines in North America, including: *Control Engineering, Industrial Distribution, Logistics Management, Manufacturing Business Technology, Modern Materials Handling, Purchasing*, and *Supply Chain Management Review*. (http://www.reedbusiness.com)

two- and four-year schools as well as vocational schools. (http://nces .ed.gov/collegenavigator)

Petersons Publisher that provides test preparation and financial aid resources in addition to an online college directory. Search by major, location, or other criteria like cost or religious affiliation. Peterson's also publishes annual college directories in print, including *Peterson's Two-Year Colleges* and *Peterson's Four-Year Colleges*. (http://www.petersons.com/ugchannel)

U.S. News and World Report Search for or view a list of the best schools in the country and search online degree programs, from both traditional colleges and from virtual schools. (http://www .usnews.com/education)

Index

A

accountant, cost, 91–92

accounting manager, 91

accreditation, college/university, 167–168

active supplier, 123

activity based costing, 123

actual cost, 123

administration/management, jobs in, 91–95

aeration, 123

Aerospace Industries Association, 157

Aerospace Manufacturing and Automated Fastening Conference and Exhibition, 53

agencies, U.S. government, 66–68

agile manufacturing, 123

agitation, 123

agribusiness, 123

AGVS. *See* automated guided vehicle system

air waybills, 145

allocations, 123

alloy, 124

amalgam, 124

American Association of Engineering Societies, 154

American Composites Manufacturers Association, 157

American Federation of Labor, 7

American Iron and Steel Institute, 157

American National Standards Institute (ANSI), 9, 65, 124

American Productivity and Quality Center (APQC), 129

American Society for Testing and Materials (ASTM), 124, 155

American Society of Safety Engineers, 154

American Society of Transportation and Logistics, 154–155

American Welding Society, 155, 160

ANSI. *See* American National Standards Institute

antitrust, 124

apparel manufacturing, 19, 37, 54

application service provider (ASP), 124

apprenticeships, 106–107, 166, 167

APQC. *See* American Productivity and Quality Center

ASP. *See* application service provider

assay, 124

assembler, 72–73

assemble to order, 124

assembling, 124

assembly

final, 135

line, 124

Association for Manufacturing Excellence, 58, 129

Association for Manufacturing Technology, 157

Association for Operations Management, 58, 155, 160

Association for the Advancement of Medical Instrumentation, 160

Association of Manufacturing Excellence, 155

Association of Manufacturing Excellence Conference, 51

associations/organizations, 154–162